The Abandoned Spouse

The
Abandoned Spouse

Jose Montserrat-Torrents

TRANSLATED AND EDITED BY
Gary MacEoin

THE BRUCE PUBLISHING COMPANY / *Milwaukee*

Preface

September, 1965 found me in Rome engaged in graduate study of the writings of the Greek Fathers of the Church, and also covering the final session of the Vatican Council for a Spanish newspaper. As were my colleagues at the press conference one day, I was amazed to learn that an Eastern-rite prelate had urged the Council Fathers to sponsor a change in canon law which would permit an innocent abandoned spouse to remarry. He was Archbishop Elias Zoghby, patriarchal vicar for Egypt of Melchite Patriarch Maximos IV Saigh, and he based his argument on a variety of quotations from the early Greek Fathers. In a very short time I was able to confirm for myself that his appeal to the authority of these Church Fathers was completely justified. I established personal contact with him and was encouraged by him to probe more deeply into the issues he had raised. I then joined forces with two Belgian Benedictines, Father Olivier Rousseau (of the Greek College in Rome) and Father Gilles de Pélichy, and the fruit of our work together was the first edition of an anthology of texts from the Greek and Roman Fathers of the Church on the issues of divorce and remarriage.

The present book has developed from the nucleus of that patristic study. The theme carried me from the Greek to the Latin Fathers, from them to the Councils of the Church, and finally—almost by way of contrast—to the teachings of theologians. Archbishop Zoghby continued, from his home in Cairo, to encourage me, and he offered me copies of the letters he had received as a result of his Council intervention. They had come

22194

from Catholics affected by current canon law in all parts of the world and they expressed in myriad languages and voices the anguish of separation and loneliness. They also testified to new hope aroused by the Archbishop's initiative and urged him to continue his efforts on their behalf. I have studied all these letters and I have extracted in Chapter 2 the testimonies I consider most characteristic and pertinent. I believe that anyone who reads them with an open mind will recognize that we have here not only the emotional response of the innocent sufferer but a moving proclamation of Christian hope and belief.

I have written this book for the general public. No specialized background is required in order to understand its message. Nevertheless, I could not overlook the fact that some of the things I was writing were new and that in consequence I would also be read by professional theologians and canonists. I was thus forced, almost instinctively, to slip back from time to time into technical language in order to express the fullness of my thought, but I am satisfied that the context is always such as to permit an adequate understanding by all readers.

It will not surprise me if some of my ideas scandalize those who make a profession out of defending orthodoxy, but that is as it should be. Everyone knows that their cries of horror are an inescapable concomitant of all progress. They are the modern equivalent of the Greek chorus underlining progress of the action and pointing out to the spectators who were half asleep in their seats that somebody on the stage had made a move.

While I was writing, I was not thinking of them, but of the innocent victims of the incongruous Catholic legislation on marriage. Some of these knew what I was doing, and their presence and hope helped me considerably to overcome the difficulties of my task. I shall never forget the hungry eyes with which they watched the pile of manuscript pages grow slowly higher. I dedicate this book principally to them.

J. M.-T.

Rome-Barcelona, April 1968

Contents

The Abandoned Spouse

CHAPTER 1

Inconsistent Marriage Laws

When priests get together, someone invariably tells a story about a bishop. It is always about a bishop somewhere else, but it is always the same story. "His technique as an administrator is incomparable," the wag will report. "It has the simplicity of genius. You could call it the two-folder system, because that is all it calls for—two folders. One is labeled 'Matters which time will resolve'; the other, 'Matters resolved by time.' The entire administrative activity is then reduced to transferring the dossiers from the one folder to the other at the appropriate moment."

As in this parable, the attitude of the Catholic Church toward problems caused by the inadequacy of its legal system for dealing with marriage cases has been to look the other way and let time resolve in favor of the law. Time, as is well known, always resolves in favor of the law, that is, until the day finally comes when it pushes the law over the cliff. Time gets rid of problems by eating up those who created them. The victim of a legal injustice rebels against it, fights, insists, get tired and dies. The law remains. And time also comes to the help of the law in another way. When the letter of the law and a tender spot of social behavior keep rubbing against each other year after year, some kind of lubricant is discovered to ease the friction and protect the dignity of the law. In this way a cohabitation is established of law and subterfuge, of privilege and counter-privilege. That is why one finds for centuries trotting alongside Catholic marriage, elbow to elbow, the institutions of divorce and prostitution, rounding the harsh edges of intransigent principle.

I

The Catholic rule of indissolubility of marriage bears permanently on its shoulders the heavy load of its secondary products, to wit, irregular marriage situations. Innumerable are the faithful Christians who suffer through no fault of their own the consequences of this inflexibility. This is a rule which inflicts equal punishment on the guilty and the innocent. To make things worse, the injustice is not marginal or accidental. It constitutes an essential part of the law as Catholic jurisprudence formulates it. The indissolubility of marriage is justified as the protector of the religious values of the conjugal union of Christians, though it is far from clear that it does so. What is perfectly clear is that it results in misfortune for thousands of innocent members of the faithful. That is its surest and most obvious effect. If we look at the situation in human terms, which is the only proper way to look at it, what we see is a legal provision designed to ensure the unhappiness of Christians under certain conditions. Its sanctifying effects are a matter of grave doubt. Its destructive efficacy, on the contrary, is absolutely certain.

I. The Nature of the Question

The problem of innocent abandoned spouses has grown in our days to such enormous dimensions that it cannot continue to be swept under the rug. It has four characteristics, and if we examine them one by one, we have no choice but to admit that this community which presents itself as the bearer of salvation for its members is face to face with a major credibility challenge.

The first characteristic of this problem is its *clarity*. The question is one that is easy to see as an urgent issue, to define and to outline. The situation of the abandoned spouse is clearly definable, distinct from other marriage situations, such as divorce or simple separation, and the fact of its presence in contemporary society is distressingly obvious. The ease with which it can be formulated puts it in a privileged position. The Church is faced today with a multitude of problems, including many serious ones, which it cannot even begin to attack because it is still searching for a way to define them. A good example is the issue of faith for man in a technological society. We agree that an acute crisis of faith exists, but we have no consensus as regards its nature or the tests to determine its presence in specified circumstances. Similarly, it is a fact that young people stay away from Church, but the explanations for their decision are many and contradictory. Although the fact is clear, its meaning and its relation to the wider issue of faith are not. No such difficulty arises as regards the problem of the innocent abandoned spouse. To mention it is to formulate it in its total depth and extension. No lengthy diagnostic procedures are required. The patient is ready to be wheeled directly into the operating theater.

Clarity is joined to *universality*. Every country in which Catholics live has men and women whose marriage situation is irregular because one spouse has abandoned the other. The substantial international community of abandoned spouses is a kind of Catholic counterpoint, the reverse of the medal, a sort of dark sign of the efficacious presence of the Church. It is beside the point that the civil laws of many countries, by allowing divorce and remarriage, lessen the social impact of such situations. The problem remains in all its acuteness at the religious and community level. The one who divorces and remarries finds himself excluded from his religious community. Statistics on the situation in some countries will be given later,[1] but they are offered simply as an illustration of the situation, and not in terms of a proof of something so obvious that it needs no proofs. The fact and its universality are alike evident.

The problem of the innocent abandoned spouse is *acute*. If we compare it with other current religious problems, its acuteness emerges as its specific internal characteristic. The situation of the abandoned spouse is a source of constant sorrow for the individual, his relatives and friends. Here we have an irregularity to which are joined suffering, desperation and sorrow. Other religious problems exhibit these characteristics at times. A crisis of faith brings suffering and grief, but the psychological pressure is not continuous. It rises and falls. Indifference in this case can enter as a psychologically liberating release. But the one who has experienced a breakdown of the conjugal union and is forbidden to build a new life by setting up another family is a prisoner of

---

[1] See Chapter 2, pp. 25f.

his problem. It weighs down on him with relentless constancy. Spiritual directors and psychiatrists alike testify to the emotional disturbances which result from the intransigence of Catholic social and legal rules regarding marriage. Sociologists report a higher level of suicides among divorced persons who have not remarried. Nor can we overlook the conflict of conscience in the believer who entered a new civil marriage after divorce. All these situations will be discussed at length in the following chapter.[2] They are mentioned here only to establish the continuing acuteness of the problem of the innocent abandoned spouse.

The problem is, finally, an *urgent* one, not only for each of the individuals who suffer it in their own flesh, but for the Christian community in general. The situation of abandoned spouses constitutes in Catholicism a stumbling block of scandal for believers, because by itself it represents a very significant part of the human sorrow provided and maintained specifically by the Church. Christians throughout the world, regardless of their denomination, have an interest in eliminating this source of irregularities from the bosom of the biggest and most widely distributed of Christian Churches. We cannot with honesty proclaim a message of freedom to those outside while within we daily witness the spectacle of so many of the faithful condemned against their will to a cruel regime of solitary isolation. When those in authority take refuge in "we cannot" in answer to the human cries of the abandoned spouse, such a confession of lack of power contradicts the spirit of the gospel of Jesus, the gospel which St. Paul proclaimed to be precisely a "we can," to be "the power of God for salvation" (Rom. 1:16).

But if the characteristics of the problem are well defined, the same is not true of the solution. Many escape routes have been proposed, with a variety of justfications for each of them. Some suggest a mere pastoral tolerance. Others would introduce divorce under changed rules of canon law. Others again opt for acceptance of civil divorce, or the abandonment of a Church discipline on marriage. The attempt to compare and evaluate all such proposals creates enormous difficulties. The fact is that all contemporary

2 See Chapter 2, pp. 27ff.

Church problems tend to be extremely complex. The most trivial decision calls for long study sessions, committees, consultations and test runs. The man in the street becomes understandably confused. He is attuned to simple and obvious solutions to the daily problems of his pragmatically-oriented life and soon asks himself if that kind of procedure is appropriate for the religious needs of this same modern man.

It is indeed obvious that the innocent abandoned spouse should be able to remarry. Centuries of accumulation of religious, dogmatic, legal and social elements, nevertheless, have transformed this plain truth into a thesis with the most intricate consequences. The human and social act of marrying was a very uncomplicated one to start. When the religious values of Christianity were woven into it, however, it came to form a single piece with all that dogmatic construction. In consequence, a change in any part produces immediate shockwaves everywhere. The question of the divorce and remarriage of Catholics overhangs the total problem of marriage at a time when both its personal and institutional dimensions are subject to profound re-evaluation, both in the area of religion and elsewhere.

In the strictly dogmatic field, the sacramentality of marriage leads of necessity to an area of theology which is bristling with controversy, the general theory of the sacraments. The theme of divorce and marriage leads later to the very topical issue of Church-world relations. Reflection on secularity cannot be left aside when one is attempting an adequate formulation of the marriage union and its breakdown. In a secularized world, the social consequences of the break-up of a marriage will not be the same as they were under the old regime when society was theocratically inspired. At the same time, it would be wrong to deny a religious element to the marriage union. To define this element precisely and determine what are or should be its consequences at a decisive moment, such as that of a break-up, is tremendously difficult both because of the enormously complicated matter itself and the constant change in attitudes. An approach with any claim to be scientific can hardly do more than offer a full view of the elements and leave the road open for whatever changes may be demanded by social and ideological progress.

The first step is to place the problem in two contexts, that of contemporary Catholicism, and that of modern anthropology. That marriage cannot be dissolved is a standard Catholic formula.[3] The expression is to be found most frequently when Catholic spokesmen are opposing divorce laws. When canon lawyers talk to each other, however, the formula is quickly followed by a whole detailed series of clarifications.

The first is to note that it applies only to Christian marriage, not to "natural" marriage. The Catholic theologian tends to sidestep the issue of the dissolubility or indissolubility of a marriage which is not a Christian sacrament. Divorce was authorized under the laws of the Old Testament, and even today the Holy See dissolves some "natural" marriages. The total effect is to limit the statement to marriages of Christians.

Not even such marriages, however, are fully covered. A long tradition recognizes that a marriage which has not been consummated can be dissolved. It is a sacrament from the moment it took place, and nevertheless it can be wiped out right up to the moment of a subsequent complete sexual union of the parties. It is consequently less than exact to say that Christian marriage cannot be dissolved.

Yet another point must still be noted. If we apply the terms used in modern civil society, we have to say that the Church courts grant real divorces in the full sense of the term. The official decision simply hides the fact under the euphemistic description of "declaration of nullity." Let us take a look at the ideological fraud which this phrase covers.

The essential element in a marriage is the loving and stable union of a man and a woman. The "consent" required by the laws of ancient Rome is found in their common life. The legal form for contracting the union, for making it a public social fact, contributes nothing to its essence. It is simply an external addition needed for the right ordering of life in society, and a guarantee of the social effects of the marriage. In the religious order, the same principles apply. The sincere giving of each partner to the other is what constitutes the religious value of

---

[3] For a fuller doctrinal development, see Chapter 5.

the marriage union. The curious legal system which subjects this religious value to certain external formal conditions appeared only quite late in the Church, and its impact is still hardly noticeable in the Catholic doctrinal teaching on marriage.

If the external legal forms have been omitted or improperly performed, the union can be dissolved. Such is the attitude of most civil codes. It is noteworthy that the common law calls such a dissolution a "divorce" pure and simple, not "a declaration of nullity." What is understood and assumed is that, in spite of the defective form, there was a true marriage, and that it is now being legally ended. The same happens when impotency or another impediment is the cause of the separation. The civil law does not invoke the fiction that the marriage never existed. It simply declares it ended for the stated reason. The fact that the spouses lived together, publicly and of their own free decision, is enough to have the union regarded in retrospect as a marriage.

Church courts (a modest plural to disguise the curious fact that there is in the entire world only one Catholic Church court —the Roman rota—for dissolving marriage) say they lack the power to dissolve a lawful consummated marriage, but that they can declare certain unions null. Defective form is the most characteristic case, and it is here used as the one that illustrates the situation most clearly. When a marriage has been contracted without the formal conditions required by the Church for validity, it can be dissolved at any time without regard for the other circumstances.

A little reflection shows what a strange rule we have here. The main constitutive element of a marriage, as already noted, is the free, loving and stable union of the spouses. This basic component is reinforced and perfected by the addition of various circumstances. The spouses live together. They share their possessions. They raise children. They establish a variety of contacts with each other's family groups and with those of their children, a development that can have major economic effects. They create a place for themselves in society. However important the legal form of the marriage contract, it is perfectly clear that it is a detail in a marriage which has acquired these other elements or even some of them. In consequence, to judge by this single marginal characteristic alone whether or not a true marriage exists is to betray an attitude of incredible superficiality. If such other elements as living together and having a family are present, although the legal form is absent or defective, the human, logical and natural thing is that the law should find a way to supply what is missing, and that is something that jurists can do almost without effort. To say that the marriage is null is to pervert human and spiritual values.

Such an approach is all the more surprising for a religious community which claims to entertain a high view of marriage and its stability. Traditional Catholic teaching in its most conservative formulations should logically lead to the rule that marriage can never be dissolved simply from a defect of form or similar circumstances. Looking at the matter from the religious viewpoint, sacramental value should be given to every union entered in good faith and with the right intentions, particularly if the marriage is subsequently confirmed by a peaceful and edifying life together. If at some point a formal defect is discovered, the juridic machinery should in all logic be put in motion to safeguard the existing values and certainly not to destroy them. The legal adjustments needed for a radical and automatic elimination of the formal defects would be elementary, and they would be totally within the spirit of the rest of current canon law. Instead, we know that Church discipline takes an altogether different direction for this single issue. Openly contradicting its strict religious and moral principles, Roman legal practice takes advantage of the tiny slit provided by defective form to rip a gap in the fence and admit divorce in the real sense.

Similar comments could be made about other causes of "declarations of nullity," though in some instances the result seems more reasonable. What is inadmissible is to keep on pretending that we are not here dealing with divorces. Impotency which existed before the marriage, for example, is recognized by all legal systems as a ground for divorce. The Roman courts also recognize it, except that they call the marriage null in that case because of the presence of a diriment impediment. When the declaration of nullity occurs after many years of living together (and crazy as it seems, after children have been born), the most honest and natural thing would simply be to call it divorce, thereby avoiding the stigma on the previous life of the parties. But the Roman authorities will have none of it. To recognize that their judicial decisions are true divorces would be to admit their power to dissolve marriage, with resulting pressures to exercise this power. Rather than yield, they prefer to live illogically.

Here then is what we find. Behind the solemn and clearcut formula proclaiming that marriage cannot be dissolved is concealed an unintelligible complex of exceptions and subterfuges which inevitably produce arbitrary and unfair results. We are encouraged, in consequence, to look for a more realistic, logical and just position, one which will not be afraid to face the issue of divorce among Christians and which will hopefully provide an answer for the problem of the abandoned spouse.

What might seem the most promising approach at first glance would be to adopt the practice of all modern states and make provision in canon law for divorce of married Christians. As was already noted, however, historical and dogmatic incrustations tend in the Catholic Church to complicate to a hopeless extent the simplest decisions. To adopt the obvious solution of admitting grounds for divorce would be to run the risk of creating a whole new set of rules according to principles that threaten soon to be out of date, to start out on a journey from which the world is already returning. Additional reflection is in order. We should examine in particular what valid new elements may be contributed by modern humanism, so that the religious values of marriage and the meaning and consequences of the break-down of marriage may be evaluated in this rich context.

II. Marriage and Divorce in Their Broader Context

Marriage in the past was studied almost exclusively in its institutional context. The decision to marry was made by the individual within a social framework which effectively limited his personal decision. Often the individual had little or nothing to say even about the choice of spouse. Marriage was a social situation, a beaten track on which all trotted along in their determined slots.

Today the situation is entirely different. Marriage as an institution takes second place to marriage as an interpersonal encounter. The institution has not, of course, disappeared from the scene, but it is now incorporated into a broader spectrum of values in which the persons themselves and their mutual relations occupy the central position. Personal elements thus have become the most important part of the marriage union. From the mutual choice and acceptance of each partner by the other to the smallest details of the life they live together, modern marriage is an expression of the free determination of a man and a woman to share their lives and complement each other mutually. The love of the spouses is the love of one person for another, not a converging esteem for a common object external to both of them, something which could be the institution of marriage or a child. The love of the spouses for each other precedes the institution, and the institution exists exclusively to protect that love and give it stability.

The result of all this is that modern man considers that marriage begins when the two people in love surrender themselves to each other lovingly, a surrender which can take place in various ways and is not necessarily limited to sexual encounter. In the social sphere, the regard for the complete freedom and independence of the marriage pact is expressed by the creation of ever quicker and easier ways to give legal standing to the unions that have formed themselves. Civil marriage has got away from the pretence of being a substitute for a religious marriage, to assume instead the nature of a formal registration of something which happened without the slightest intervention on the part of the authorities.

The eminently interpersonal nature of the union of the parties has a direct bearing also on the conditions for ending that union. When love has disappeared without leaving a trace of mutual esteem or a desire to continue to live together in harmony, the union of the man and woman loses the dignity of an action freely performed and becomes instead social constraint supported by the dead weight of the institution. The marriage has gone and only the appearances survive. Separation of the parties

and divorce are now merely a recognition of an irreversible
fact.

Separation and divorce will be avoided at times for such reasons as the harm that others, particularly the children, can suffer.
Agreement in such terms can provide for the spouses a new
way to live together and to relate to each other, and here again
we have an expression of their freedom and of their desire to
perfect themselves. In other cases, it will prove impossible to
live together, and even the children will benefit when the parents separate.

Even in such circumstances, nevertheless, it is not the function
of the public authority to determine whether or not an adequate reason exists for the break. Rather, the collapse of the
marriage is presented as an established fact, and the duty of
the delegates of society is limited to placing it on the public
record. This does not mean, however, that society should accept every separation without question and grant a divorce indiscriminately to anyone who asks it. A divorce pronounced by
the civil authority affects the legal and public status of a marriage and not its internal nature. The judge does not declare that
a marriage has been dissolved but that its dissolution—with all
the necessary consequences—is acceptable in the juridic order.

This precise formulation of the social and personal elements
in marriage, the two aspects here outlined, is of the highest importance when we begin to study their effect on the religious
evaluation of the conjugal union.

Theological speculation insists on identifying the introduction
of the religious values of marriage with the legal acts which
constitute a contract.[4] Although it is recognized in theory that
"the ministers of the sacrament are the contracting parties," in
actual fact their action is completely conditioned by the formal
circumstances.

If, however, marriage is to continue to have a religious meaning for modern man, such meaning cannot be rooted in an external and strictly formal action, nor can it depend on such an

---

[4] See Chapter 5, pp. 129ff.

action alone. Nothing less than the community of husband and wife as an interpersonal relationship will suffice to provide the new transcendent dimension which will make of the expression of human love a real presence of divine love in the faith of the believer. The married Christian does not have to split himself schizophrenically between two loves, because he can find divine love simply by deepening the affection which unites him to his spouse. And this is precisely where the reification of the theory of the sacraments produces disastrously negative results. The sacrament is understood as a "thing" of the divine order added to the "natural" reality of the marriage. This supernatural thing is presented to the amazed eyes of the spouses with a wealth of detail. They are told when it is given and when it is not given, the exact moment when it appears, how it languishes and how it revives, how it increases and how it acts. Without this "thing," every loving union between a Christian man and woman is reduced to the level of shameful concubinage. In a word, the sacrament is defined by the juridic act of the contract.

For those who have a personalist view of human relations, the anthropological poverty of the contract-sacrament formulation is highly distressing. But the speculative inadequacy of the current Catholic description of marriage does not stop there. The very name of sacrament hides a conceptual ambiguity which urgently needs to be clarified if we want marriage to continue to retain a religious meaning for Christians who belong to our modern world.

For eight centuries, Catholic theology has been a slave to a generic religious category established and imposed in virtue of the platonic dogmas of the reality of ideas and of the way humans share in them, namely, the "sacrament." Progressively developed by successive theologians, this concept finally was raised to the status of an absolute, polarizing around it all speculation concerning the communication of God to man. For better or worse, the rich variety of religious forms created by Christianity was narrowed down to fit in the rigid molds of the sacramental theory, a theory constructed on the analogy of baptism and explained in terms of aristotelian metaphysics. By this means, Catholicism achieved the most complete religious system of reification of the transcendent. But at the same time, it impoverished significantly the broad sweep of the relations of God with men by spelling out a detailed program of the times and places in which such an encounter might occur. Once that was done, it was easy to progress to all kinds of picturesque embellishments, from the effort to identify a matter and a form in marriage all the way to mathematical tabulations for determining the quantity of grace received by the believer.

What has been said is not intended to suggest that the sacramental theory of marriage is substantially false, but simply that it is poor and inadequate. Today, we have different anthropological perspectives, and we must adjust ourselves to their demands in our explanations of the religious meaning of marriage. The diagrammatic presentation of reified transcendency has become totally unacceptable, and the only language still meaningful is that of interpersonal communication. The stress is on the person and on relations between persons. Any "object" outside of and apart from these components has ceased to be important.

In this broader context the problems of marriage breakdown and divorce begin to make sense. Within the speculative description of reification, matrimony could be reasonably presented as indissoluble, because the "thing" continued to hold the spouses together in a higher community even after they were physically and emotionally separated. The individual was seen as a lower ontological category and consequently bound by the demands of transcendent realities. The platonic world has, however, long since disappeared. Marriage is not a participation in some heaven of unalterable realities. Once the persons have separated and love has disappeared, absolutely nothing survives. Neither children nor legal fictions suffice to maintain the existence of the marriage. The only thing to do is to recognize the breakdown and give legal recognition to the separation. The love which has been destroyed by the inadequacy or wrong doing of one or both parties can try once more to find its realization in a new direction. Sociologists insist that second marriages tend to be far more stable than the first tries.

All efforts to justify the indissolubility of marriage on the grounds of its religious or "sacramental" character should, consequently, be abandoned. Man is the carrier of religious values, and man also causes them to decay. By itself, the sacrament of marriage no more makes a man married than does baptism make a Christian of one who does not love Christ. Nor is that all. The religious value of the marital union, precisely because it is rooted in what is noblest in human love, can disappear long before the union itself. Extrinsic motives or social conventions can maintain the community of married life, but if there is no free mutual giving in love, the living together lacks all religious meaning. Divine things are not so easy to arrange as the medieval theologians thought.

The conclusion that seems to flow from this series of super-imposed reflections is that the Catholic Church should admit the dissolubility of marriage and promulgate an adequate divorce code. Such, at least, is the direction in which most Catholic thinkers favorable to divorce are moving. But other possibilities also exist. As already noted, the issues involved in Christian marriage are extremely complex, being tied in with many other aspects of social and religious life. A deeper reflection on them suggests that we have not yet necessarily reached final conclusions. Marriage has always been a point of contention between the Church and the world. The struggle has continued so long, with the battle lines fluctuating wildly in both directions, that the basic claims of each party are no longer easy to disentangle. What is now urgently needed is to subject the issues to impartial examination. And before we can pronounce definitely on the place of marriage and divorce in the Church, it is necessary to determine precisely the place of the Church in the world.

III. MARRIAGE IN A SECULARIZED WORLD

In his film "Deus e o diabo na terra do sol" (God and the devil in the land of the sun), the Brazilian director Glauber Rocha describes the exploits of a holy man and of a bandit operating in the arid backlands, then ends his hair-raising tales of a blind man with the observations: "The moral of all this is that the land belongs neither to God nor to the devil, but to man."

Today's Christian can subscribe in good conscience to the thesis of the storyteller of the *sertao*, namely, that the devil is a fiction and God gave the earth to man. Formerly, man—as a stranger in his homeland—merely played the part of observer and chronicler of the tremendous struggles enacted before his eyes by the spirits of good and the spirits of evil, by the gods and the demons. All human realities were marked with the sign of one or other of the contenders. To the devil belonged such things as illness, sin, death, the earthquake and the hurricane. In the sphere of the divine, on the other hand, were listed life, virtue, victory over one's enemies, poetic inspiration and marriage.

Thanks to a long process of liberation, man has progressively acquired consciousness of his freedom and independence, as well as of his autonomy vis-à-vis every kind of supraterrestrial power. Step by step, man has humanized his environment by expelling gods and demons from the affairs of this world. The world acquired an identity as such, or—as we say today—it became secularized.

The process of secularization need not be described here. It is sufficient to mention it in order to insert into it one of the most important of human realities, namely, marriage. As an integral part of the great sacred cycle of generation and life, marriage has over the centuries been constantly molded by religious influences. In the perspective of an all-absorbing transcendence, the man and woman ceased to be the protagonists in their own marriage and became instead supporting actors in a spectacular performance of cosmic dimensions. Our era restores its genuine worldly quality to marriage. There is nothing in the marital union which transcends the persons who form it. The value of the marriage is strictly limited to the persons and their mutual relationship. Any imaginary transcendent reality which it is sought to incorporate into this living context breaks down into alienation and degenerates into a myth.

On the institutional and social level marriage does indeed acquire a certain meaning, but this new dimension does not remove it from its purely worldly condition. Marriage as a social institution consists simply of the complex of rules and juridic pro-

visions which regulate and protect the right of individuals to
marry. The marriage as such does not become identified with
the institution but receives from it a purely external addition.
Every effort to bring pressure to bear on the conjugal community through institutional demands shows up as an abuse
which contemporary man rightly rejects. Yet this is precisely
the misleading way in which medieval Catholic tradition has
sought to impose controls on marriage.

Marriage as a social and religious institution is an effort to
bring the whole of the legal order of marriage under Church
control. But, as I have already noted, the entire thrust of modern
man is toward a complete rejection of absorbing and controlling
objectivizations of the transcendent. The demands of the institution bring no values in the religious sphere or in any other to
marriage. The only source of religious meaning in marriage is
to be sought exclusively in the one element which can establish
religious values in the world, namely, the human person. Every
free and personal act of man can be performed in a religious
context. The mutual giving of the spouses can take place religiously. The Church can point out the content of this religious meaning and propose it to its members. What it cannot
do is to place religious conditions on a human act. According
to the vitality of their faith and the state of their consciences,
the spouses will live the religious value of their union or will
fail to do so. But any reification of this value and subsequent
transformation into a legal prescription will be energetically
rejected in the name of the autonomy of the human person. To
sum up the true situation, in the marriage union of Christians,
the Christian element is not the marriage but the persons who
are joined in marriage.

In consequence, there is no reality that can be properly described as the institution of Christian marriage. On the institutional level, marriage pertains integrally to the secular order.
There is no place for anything comparable to a legal religious
statute of marriage. Competence in this field pertains exclusively
to the human community. Religious groups should do no more
than accept the legal order and marriage customs in the many

and changing forms in which they are found, with no right to intervene beyond that of every member of the community to act on matters of public concern.

One this viewpoint is accepted, the specific Catholic problem regarding divorce and the abandoned spouse all but disappears. There is no longer any need to introduce provisions for divorce into canon law. The competence of the Church to determine the validity, the possibility or the legality of a marriage or of a divorce no longer exists. The ministers of the Church should not pronounce on separations because they should not pronounce on unions. If the discipline and canonical form of marriage has disappeared, there is no place for a discipline and canonical form of divorce. Christians will unite in marriage and separate according to the laws and customs of the various human communities, following the freely observed dictates of their own consciences. The religious communities will limit their role to acceptance of the civil status of the spouses. This will not imply an abandonment of their own moral standards but merely a recognition that those standards are not to be expressed in juridic norms. What characterizes moral religious standards is precisely the fact that they are limited to the realm of the individual conscience.

In this context, the situation of the abandoned Catholic spouse no longer presents itself as a specific problem. The parties who have separated will get a civil divorce, after which they can marry again if they so desire. The religious community will play no part in this process and will accept the new situations without questioning them. Every party involved in the events leading to the separation will know in his own conscience the extent of his guilt. More specifically, he will be conscious of the effects in the religious sphere of his awareness of his guilt. The state of his conscience, however, bears no relation to his legal situation.

The social institutions of marriage and divorce will depend in a secularized world on purely human conditioning and motivation, without any interference from organized religion. The human element alone is able to unite men. Faced with the choices that will arise in his married life, the Christian will decide on the basis of criteria he shares with all the other members of society, since this is the only way to ensure that he will no longer feel himself a stranger in the common homeland.

The sacred values which Christianity has discovered through a long process of reflection in the community of marriage must be reformulated to fit these premises. The sacramentality of Christian marriage must be given a more personalist explanation so that it can continue to be a source of spiritual self-discovery for those who live it, without the need for alienation into forms of pseudo-religious objectivization. Once this starting-point is accepted, any attempt to regulate the social order of marriage on the basis of transcendent motivations will be seen as abusive, and the human community will do well to take a firm stand against it.

IV. The Range of Practical Solutions

The principle of the secularity of the institution of marriage, as presented above, is offered throughout this book as a mere postulate. Not many Catholics accept this postulate today, but it is beginning to gain ground in Christian ecumenical reflection.

The postulate of secularity eliminates completely all the problems resulting from the inadequacy of current Church discipline regarding marriage. The fact must, however, be faced that such a basic elimination is in the present climate little better than utopian. By seeking to resolve everything, this procedure in practice resolves nothing today. It is consequently necessary to get back to common ground and study the problems of divorce and remarriage on the basis of universally accepted theological and canonical principles, and that is what this book will attempt. What has already been said about the complex intertwining of the issues shows the difficulty of the undertaking. But our first reflections offer a sure guideline. Catholic teaching on marriage, as seen in its origins and development, recognizes the possibility of divorce and remarriage in certain circumstances, and the situation of the innocent abandoned spouse occupies a place of particular privilege among those circumstances.

Even at this level, nevertheless, strong resistance is encountered. The trend of the theologians of the Roman Curia has been in recent times toward a pure and simple acceptance of canonical divorce, but the doctrinal elements for such a renewal are still in the embryonic state. What is worse, nobody is willing to discuss the issues in public, due in large part to the peculiar conditions of Italian politics. It becomes necessary, in consequence, to present a provisional solution that will at least take care of the serious and pressing problem, the situation of the innocent abandoned spouse. This is the reason why the practical proposal to be presented later has little or nothing to do with the broad principles and conclusions that would flow from a logical pursuit of the question in the terms proposed in this first chapter.[5] The purpose is to present a provisional and marginal solution, one that will resolve a great number of currently hopeless situations without changing excessively the framework of existing law. Acceptance of a proposal of this kind will undoubtedly increase even further the present incoherence of Catholic legislation on marriage. But this is what happens with all legal systems that have survived their usefulness. Before they disappear completely, they exist for a time buried under a mass of corrections and emergency revisions intended to direct the impetuous flow of social life in a determined direction. Such a solution is purely provisional, but it is better than none. What is unacceptable is to ignore the new needs and keep the unworkable old rules in full force, shielding oneself behind the rusty excuses of sacred untouchability.

To sum up, it is proposed to study four very different aspects of Catholic discipline regarding marriage and divorce. In order to avoid as far as possible the ambiguities of expression which necessarily flow from so complicated a survey, it is desirable to summarize the characteristics of each of these four situations.

1. The present system gives marriage between Christians the nature of a sacred institution. In consequence, it falls almost entirely under the jurisdiction of the Church. Once marriage is entered into canonically and consummated physically, the Church declares it to be indissoluble and consequently refuses to authorize or permit the divorce of such spouses. If one spouse

---

[5] Developed in Chapter 6, pp. 167–182.

is abandoned, even without any blame on his part, the marriage continues to be regarded as valid, and the injured party is not permitted in any circumstances to remarry. If he turns to the civil authorities for a divorce and remarriage, he is proclaimed a public sinner and excluded from the religious life of his community. The only choice offered the abandoned Catholic spouse is compulsory celibacy. In addition, the teaching authorities of the Church continue to denounce civil divorce, in spite of the fact that it is recognized by almost all civilized states.

The intolerable situation of innocent abandoned spouses has caused the appearance, at the pastoral level, of a variety of palliatives. More well-intentioned than reasonable, they all boil down to a toleration in practice of violations of the law, a clear sign that the system is tottering.[6]

2. Theologians and canonists are racking their brains to find a solution by means of a new application of the universally accepted principle that the Church has jurisdiction over marriage. The most progressive urge a straightforward admission of various grounds for divorce. Others, more cautious, suggest further extension of the grounds already recognized in order to bring a long list of additional situations under the old umbrella of "lack of consummation" and "defective form." In their view, a divorce on grounds of incompatibility could be given in the form of a declaration of nullity for lack of consummation, understanding this term in a broader sense.[7]

The reason for the theological difficulty of a "canonical divorce" is that such a category has never existed in the Catholic tradition of the West. The survey of tradition presented in a later chapter does indeed show that the Church admitted certain cases of divorce. At the time in question, however, there was no intervention of the Church authorities either in the marriage or in its dissolution. What was at issue was a purely civil act. Many theologians who accept with great difficulty the power of the Church to "marry" ecclesiastically have the good

---

6 See pp. 181f.
7 Different solutions along these lines are offered in Chapter 5, p. 146.

sense to deny to the Church the power to "unmarry." "Religious divorce" is an expression offensive to their ears.

3. The blind alley of Catholic divorce suggests a nuanced return to the situation that existed before the introduction of the ecclesiastical-theocratic system.[8] Marriage, both in its making and its unmaking, is a purely human fact, or as the theologians like to say, "natural." This is what has been called above the secularity of the institution of marriage. In accordance with this principle, the marriage and the divorce of Christians will be governed by the civil laws of each country, without interference of any kind by the religious authorities. The Church would drop completely its laws and regulations governing marriage and would limit itself to teaching the religious values of the union of the sexes in a perspective that would focus exclusively on the personal life of the Christian. This approach, although it is quite foreign to the current thinking of Church authorities, seems to be the one indicated by the signs of the time.

4. Within the framework of the process of secularization, it is possible to foresee the rapid introduction of one change that would not upset excessively the existing Church structures, and the practical proposal made in this book is based on that premise. The suggestion is that we should begin to recognize the Christian legitimacy of certain civil divorces and remarriages for a particular group of Christians, namely, those who have been abandoned by their spouses through no fault of their own. The new marriage of the divorced Catholic in this category would be automatically considered as on a par with canonical marriage, even though no action had been taken by the ecclesiastical authorities. In the life of the religious community, no distinction would be made between such a marriage and a marriage under Church law.

The following chapters must be read in the light of these four situations, the reason being that a study of the historic and dogmatic background brings to light now one and now another of the situations just described. The evolution of theological

[8] See the conclusions drawn in Chapters 3 and 4, pp. 79 and 120f.

and canonical teaching on Catholic marriage is irregular and organically disjointed. Because of this, most of what follows is analytical. It has proved necessary to examine the diverse and varied aspects of the question point by point in order to establish the extent to which the demands for a solution are reasonable. In these introductory pages, nevertheless, an effort has been made to present a theoretic view of the whole, despite the risk of oversimplification. Such a theoretic view will give the reader a set of principles with which to judge and understand what follows. In this way, too, there is less danger of the work turning out to be useless. Even if the conclusions are judged unacceptable in some quarters, a study of the data can still provide elements for new proposals and practical suggestions which may lead to a quick and final resolution of the very serious problem of the innocent abandoned spouse.

CHAPTER 2

The Voice of the Abandoned

Any reader can undoubtedly, by checking around in his own neighborhood, list at least half a dozen broken marriages of Catholics which have led to divorce, separation, the return of a wife to her parents' home, the abandonment of a mother with young children, the creation of a situation involving exclusion from the Catholic community, and so on. In these circumstances, it would be a waste of time to set out to demonstrate that the problem exists. Everyone has positive proof in his own backyard that it is both common and serious. The present chapter, accordingly, will merely formulate the extent of the problem and list its principal characteristics. It will then be possible to proceed with more confidence to the historical and doctrinal study, and to point to the direction in which a solution can be found.

The first step is to clarify the precise limits of the study. As its title indicates, it is concerned only with the situation of the innocent abandoned spouse, whether remarried or not. There are many reasons for this limitation. The main one is that the case of the abandoned spouse presents a situation which is both very characteristic and clearly distinguished from others in the social, moral and religious sphere.

Another valid reason for the distinction is that the problems of the innocent party, as distinguished from those of the guilty one, permit a religious and theological treatment; or to be more precise, they demand such a treatment. The innocent abandoned spouse remains for a longer or shorter time within the Catholic community, appealing for help and demanding a solution for his problems. The guilty party, on the other hand, takes the initiative in leaving his religious group. He usually makes no effort to regularize his relationship with this group until much later, when advanced age, illness or the death of the other party has so altered the circumstances as to facilitate a formal reincorporation. The Catholic community consequently includes many members who suffer as a result of a marriage breakdown for which they feel themselves in no way responsible, a fact which by itself fully justifies the purposes of this work.

To speak of an "innocent" party may give rise to some misinterpretations. The experience of moralists and of those who deal with marriage cases shows that it is very hard to allocate the blame for the breakdown, and that as a rule both spouses share responsibility for failure. Accepting this as a fact, it in no way affects the validity of the approach. The present study starts from the position that every Catholic community includes abandoned or separated spouses who say that they were not to blame and who are accepted by the community on that basis. The evidence and the legal criteria for establishing the truth of their assertion are here beside the point. In point of fact, the some 200 letters received by Archbishop Zoghby were all written by persons who claimed that they were not to blame for the breakdown of their marriages. Even if only these 200 were helped, the effort of writing this book would be more than justified.

The purpose of the present chapter is to analyze the seriousness, the extent, and the characteristics of the problem. When dealing with the extent, some statistics are included, though without giving them excessive weight. It seems more useful to place the primary stress on the large number of authentic testimonies which are reproduced. They not only establish but describe in photographic detail the different situations encountered and the many aspects of the question.

The only statistics available give numbers of separated or divorced Catholics without distinguishing guilt or innocence and without determining how many have remarried. Nobody has attempted to make a count which would list these various elements, and in consequence the figures here presented are the result of extrapolations and indirect calculations.

In the United States, the annual rate of divorce has remained constant at 2.2 per thousand inhabitants since 1962.[1] The proportion of divorced Catholics may be lower than the national average, although the gap between the two is narrowing steadily. This means that about 70,000 Catholic marriages in the United States end each year in divorce. If we assume an average life span of 30 years after divorce, we reach a figure of 4,200,000 divorced Catholics.[2]

Analyzing the figures provided by the 1950 census, Glick has reached the conclusion that in the United States two-thirds of divorced women and all divorced men remarry.[3] By comparing the data in the "Statistical Abstracts of the United States for 1965" and those in the "Official Catholic Directory for the United States," Pospishil came up with a figure of 68,000 Catholics married each year outside the Church.[4]

These figures must be increased significantly when it is remembered that many separations are not formalized. A Catholic sociologist has calculated that of every hundred broken Catholic marriages only 40 are carried through the divorce courts.[5]

Even allowing for a substantial margin of error in these statistical projections, one fact remains clear. The situation of a considerable number of Catholic marriages in the United States is irregular. The general estimate of one in ten does not seem exaggerated.[6]

Substantially the same situation exists in other countries. Divorces in the Federal German Republic totaled 49,521 in 1962,

---

[1] Data for the United States from Pospishil's *Divorce and Remarriage* (New York: Herder & Herder, 1967). He cites many sources and combines them skillfully. The statistic quoted here is found on p. 84, note 1. It comes from a U.S. Public Health Service source.

[2] Pospishil, *op. cit.*, p. 85.

[3] Glick, *American Families*, p. 139. Pospishil, *op. cit.*, p. 86.

[4] Pospishil, *op. cit.*, pp. 87–88.

[5] Alves, p. 203.

[6] "The combined figure of all existing families which are socially in conflict or disrupted is probably around 10 per cent. . . . Their number is much greater than is generally recognized by the community or by professional persons." Thomas P. Monahan, quoted by Pospishil, *op. cit.*, p. 89.

nearly one half of them involving Catholic spouses.[7] The French courts process about 30,000 divorces every year. The number of legal or de facto separations comes to 40,000 a year in Italy, according to calculations made by Sansone and Nenni in 1958, and to 67,000 according to those of *La Stampa* in 1954.[8] A conservative deduction from these various statistics and estimates is that ten per cent of Catholic marriages throughout the world are irregular.

Our witnesses, however, are not going to be numbers but persons. Figures are cold. When applied to human problems, they can produce amazingly ambiguous results. Direct testimony is far more valuable in a work that approaches problems in a religious perspective. The figures have already expressed all they are capable of saying, namely, that the problem of Catholic spouses who have separated and remarried exists, and that it is a major problem. What is now needed is to refine the problem, to study its many aspects and to show how often it occurs within a religious context. This will be done by means of 40 testimonies, all written in 1965 and 1966, selected from the 200 received by Archbishop Zoghby. As stipulated by the Archbishop, they will be reproduced in a form that hides the identity and personal circumstances of the writers. The facts of each case, however, remain. What is presented is not a fictitious situation but one that is unhappily real in some part of the world.

I. The Diversity of the Situations

Abandonment creates different social, psychological, and religious situations according to the person and the circumstances. A mature woman with dependent children presents problems which are primarily social and economic. A young man whose wife has left him is likely to find himself in a tensely dramatic personal situation with serious psychological overtones. Remarriage of a divorced believer raises acute religious conflicts. Each situation has its own sociological framework, and the different

[7] H. Flatten, *Das Aergernis der Kirchlichen Eheprozesse* (Paderborn, Schöningh, 1965), p. 15.
[8] Fortuna-Jorio-Pandini, p. 33.

characteristics can best be identified by presenting a series of actual cases.

The statistics show that an overwhelming majority of the separated and the divorced remarry, either licitly or illicitly. Cases nevertheless exist of absolute fidelity to the iron canon law of indissolubility. Even if they are not numerous, they are significant. They stress the unhappy choices offered the abandoned spouse—remarriage outside the Church or a constant threat of emotional imbalance.

A letter from France presents a situation that was very common in the postwar years. "It seems to me fully logical that those who have been forced to accept a divorce should be able to marry again in the Church and receive the sacraments. Let me give you the example of one of our relatives. He is a young man who married during the Indochina war and became the father of a daughter. When he got home from the war, he discovered that his wife had left him and was going to have a child by another man. The divorce decree placed the entire blame on the wife and gave him custody of their child.

"Last winter, this man met a very serious young woman and wanted to marry her, but she was not willing to settle for anything but a Church wedding. The misfortune is that this girl comes from a very good family and would have given the child an excellent upbringing.

"I accordingly think it is very sad that one has to suffer for a lifetime and remain always under a public stigma. If there were any logic, a widow or a widower would not be able to remarry either, because this reasoning would make marriage indissoluble even in the grave. . . ."

The Italian civil code creates situations that would be laughable if it were not for the anguish they cause to their innocent victims. A letter from a breezy young Italian man describes one such.

"I married August 30, 1959, and all went well until late 1963. I then realized that my wife was leading a double life, and I urged her without success to end her cheating. On December 15 I asked her to go to live with her brother a short distance from our home. Still hopeful that she would mend her ways, I went to see her as often as I could, and I did everything in my power to make peace with her. At the end of three months, however, she fought with her brother also and went off I neither know where nor with whom.

"A few days ago I received a letter from the Section of Maternity and Infants asking me to call. I had learned that my wife was living with a family, and I went to see what had happened to her. Imagine my surprise to learn from her that she was going to have another child after 14 months of separation, and that—according to the law—I was the father. At this point I have to ask myself if there is not some way to change such laws. Whoever is to blame, divorce is legal in all parts of the world.

"I am still young, just 31 years of age, and am I to be in a prison without walls for the rest of my life just because I made the mistake of saying yes? It only takes a fraction of a second to say, and am I to be condemned without appeal? It seems, nevertheless, that I am not the only one caught in this trap. I have discovered that hundreds and perhaps thousands in Italy alone are in a like situation. Why does this happen only in Italy?"

The impressive document that follows is presented with all its details by the express permission of the writer who in 1965 authorized a member of a French religious order to make it public in its entirety.

Three months after his marriage in 1939, Paul left for the war and Isabelle went to live with her parents. Within a short time, Paul was taken prisoner by the Germans. A shell struck his home, killing his father and causing his mother to lose a leg. All through his imprisonment, he wrote loving letters to his wife, and she replied with equal tenderness. Four months before Paul's return to France, however, Isabelle gave birth to a son. It was only when he reached his mother's home that he learned the dreadful news. Three days later, he wrote as follows to his wife.

"Isabelle, my only love. I arrived on Thursday, to discover that the Swastika had destroyed all I held dear. My father is gone. My mother is an invalid. I no longer have a home, and I was about to add that neither do I have a wife. But no, Isabelle, I cannot believe that this liberation to which I had looked forward with such eagerness has nothing more to offer me than a chalice of bitterness. I return with my health. I still have faith. I cannot believe that God created me only to make me a martyr. Mamma has told me everything. Yours is a human weakness, my love, and let the one who never sinned cast the first stone. You have given birth to a son who bears my name and who will be our first born. I swear to you that our married life will start again with the same love as before. I forgive you all, and I don't want to know anything whatever about what happened from the day we parted until the day we resume the honeymoon interrupted by Hitler. Just let me know, my sweet Isabelle, where I can meet you. During the hell of my imprisonment I made a vow that our first trip would be a Te Deum at Lourdes. I don't want to postpone it a minute longer than I have to. Telephone me at the above number just as soon as you get this letter. I want to hold you in my arms. Love from your Paul."

The telephone did not ring. Instead, Paul got this reply.

"My very dear Paul. I am able to repeat your letter with my eyes closed. And by now, nobody could read what it says, because the writing has all been washed away by my tears.

"Words do not exist to describe my conduct. For years I kept my promise, and I fell only when I was rejoicing at the prospect of your return. You are very good, Paul, to forgive me. How many times I thought of killing myself while I was pregnant! You cannot even imagine. But I did not wish to die as a criminal, for to kill myself would mean also to kill the infant in my womb.

"You tell me, Paul, that you have drunk the chalice to the dregs. Can I ask more of you? Forget about me. I am unworthy to be your wife. Never, never could I look you in the eyes. And every time that my child would call you Papa, a thorn would be driven deeper and deeper into my heart. Besides, he has to know the truth one day, and what would he think then of his mother?

"Paul, I have thought everything over carefully and reached

a clear decision during my sleepless nights. I have no choice. I must marry the father of my child. In spite of your goodness, I have no right to impose on you the fruit of my misconduct. I have talked it over with him, and he agrees. We shall go to live in another country, and you will make a new home for yourself.

"Now, Paul, one great final favor to prove your love and your forgiveness. Please spare me the confrontation with a view to reconciliation before the judge. Everything has been my fault. I leave you whatever I brought as dowry, and I shall pay all the costs of the divorce. I want, my Paul, to retain the memory of our 'au revoir' which fate has turned into a 'good-bye.' Isabelle."

Paul, his heart broken, had no choice but to agree. Isabelle was remarried in a civil ceremony. Her husband, a diplomat, transferred to an overseas post. They now have three children. Paul, a medical doctor by profession, lives as a bachelor because that is the only thing he can do. He spent a long period of recuperation in a rest home after Isabelle's departure, then undertook specialized studies with the intention of forgetting his own problems. He has since had several opportunities to start a new life, but because he could not offer the woman he loved a Church marriage, he has decided to consecrate himself totally to his medical talent. This man, who carries in his heart a pain for which nobody can provide a cure, spends his time curing the physical ailments of others. Every possible angle has been explored in vain with the top lawyers of the Roman Rota. The answer, as expressed by one of its judges, is final. "There is no possible way to remarry in the Church."

The friend of Paul and Isabelle who reported these facts to the French priest, concluded with the following comments.

"I do not hide from you, reverend Father, the fact that such intransigence on the part of the Church has upset me most profoundly. I accept the law of the indissolubility of the marriage bond. But the Church has been given the power to bind and to loose on earth, and what I want to know is why it cannot find room in the law for exceptions. Nobody is responsible for the faults of others, as long as he has not made himself an accomplice. What would you think, reverend Father, of a judge who found a man guilty because his wife was to blame? Yet that is precisely the obnoxious role in which the intransigence of the Church places the Supreme Judge, the all-wise and all-loving God who is by definition infinitely good and infinitely just. Such an attitude on the part of the Church justifies the disregard and the hatred felt by some thinkers for the mere idea of God. Did Christ not say, 'Come to me, all you who suffer. . . .'? How can that call of Christ be applied to my friend Paul, since his suffering is incurable?

"I should deeply appreciate, reverend Father, a word from you. I see Paul several times a year. I consider him a saint, and I am sure that the Church in the course of the centuries has canonized many who possessed strength like his. I also maintain excellent relations with Isabelle. We write each other from time to time. She, for her part, suffers because she cannot receive the sacraments. Nevertheless, she is an admirable mother. With her 'husband,' she makes an ideal home. . . ."

The abandoned spouse who lives a celibate life is, nevertheless, an exception, and this is particularly true in countries which recognize civil divorce, as most countries now do. In the survey mentioned earlier, Glick found that in the United States a hundred per cent of divorced men intend to marry again. He also established that second marriages tend to be highly stable, and also that the average time from divorce to remarriage is 30 months.[9] On the basis of Detroit's divorce statistics for 1952, William J. Goode says that second marriages tend to be happier, particularly in the case of Catholics.[10]

The next three letters, one from Belgium and the other two from Italy, describe the situation of the abandoned spouse who can contract a new civil marriage and the still harsher lot of those who can set up a new home only on the official basis of "concubinage" because the state does not sanction divorce.

"In 1939," wrote the correspondent from Belgium, "my son-in-law was mobilized, and he spent the next four years as a prisoner of war. He had been married just three months when

[9] Glick, *op. cit.*, p. 198.
[10] Goode, p. 11; Pospishil, *op. cit.*, p. 86.

he was called up. While he was a prisoner in Germany, his wife was unfaithful to him. He succeeded in having her caught in the act of adultery and he was granted a divorce.

"On his return to Belgium, he met my eldest daughter, aged 25, and they became fond of each other. My family was deeply Catholic, so that for me it was very hard to face the situation and give my consent. I consulted several priests. They were sorry, but all they could do was to advise against the proposed marriage. However, they went ahead, with the result that my very devout daughter can no longer fulfill her religious duties, much as she would like to. They have had three children, one of whom has died.

"To come to the point, I am convinced from all my reading that there are many angles to this question. It is clear that the Church cannot make a man who has been divorced through no fault of his own live a celibate life. He must live in the world, and his life is very different from that of the priest who has taken a vow of chastity. I accordingly offer this as a typical case, and I want to add the comment that I think it is somewhat hypocritical to try to bury the matter under a few handfuls of clay. It is like saying that we should close our eyes and not discuss the issue further. . . ."

The two Italians were also prisoners of war. The first, who describes himself as a good citizen and an excellent worker, says he was mobilized in 1941. He was then aged 21 and married. "In 1942 I was taken prisoner and was not released until 1945. During these years, although I continued to write to my wife, she chose to betray me. When I was repatriated, we separated legally, and each of us started a new family. In the eyes of the Church and of the state, however, my new partner and I are not husband and wife. Do you not think that the veterans of a war that went on for too long should have the right to regain the liberty which we lost through no fault of our own?"

The other Italian writes at greater length. "I have been unfortunate in my marriage. I married for love in 1938, was mobilized two years later, and taken prisoner in Greece in 1941. I was released only in 1946, but during all those years I kept in touch with my wife and she wrote to me. Nevertheless, she chose to betray me. So what was I to do on my return after a long harsh and humiliating imprisonment of 5 years and 3 months? I could not stoop to trickery to obtain my complete freedom, so I had to be satisfied with a legal separation. I love children and home life, so I started a new family with a very fine girl. Our two children, aged 15 and 10, go regularly to school, and I have found here what I was unjustly denied in my first marriage. We are very fond of each other, and I think there is nothing more beautiful in the world than to love each other both in the family and outside. Nevertheless, I am in violation of the law by this marriage, and I am concerned for my children who do not yet know that their mother and I are not husband and wife. I had hoped that in 20 years the law would be changed some way, at least to legitimate the children. My first wife has also formed a new family, so that we have two families outside the law. Here I want to make a comment, and you must forgive me if I overstep. The Church should do something for all those unhappy situations you told me about. I have nothing against the Church. I need it, just as it needs us. There are thousands like me in Italy, and the Church cannot and should not ignore us. You are absolutely wonderful, and please forgive this outburst which comes from a humble son anxious to serve the Church."

Separated or divorced women who have not remarried constitute an acute pastoral problem. Their number is considerable. Glick, as noted above, says that two-thirds of divorced women remarry. The other third forms the legion of those who live alone, often with children, and nearly always in an extremely unstable social and economic situation.

The French bishops recently took note of this group. In a publication entitled "Divorced persons who have not remarried and separated women,"[11] they analyze the economic difficulties, the psychological situation, and the potential for help of the Christian community. Catholic authors who discuss divorce usu-

---

[11] *La Documentation Catholique*, 64 (1967), col. 1711–1716.

ally refer in passing to this problem. Their practical recommendations usually bring to mind a doctor who prescribes aspirin for cancer.[12]

Two letters describe the reality. The first is from the United States. "My daughter is one of these. She was deserted six and a half years ago while in the third month of pregnancy. Her husband has made no effort to see the child—when last heard of, he was in California—who is supported by my daughter with the help of her father and me. We love the child, but it is a very sad life for my daughter who at thirty-one years of age sees so many of her friends getting so much out of living.

"While I look with disgust on people who plan remarriage at the same time they get divorced, I feel that something could be done to help people in my daughter's situation. Perhaps a time lapse of several years following a desertion could be used as a standard to set aside a marriage decree and permit remarriage."

The second letter is from Venezuela. "After three years of marriage, my husband left our son and me to live with another woman, and they now have children of their own. As a Catholic, I told my story to the bishop. He talked to my husband and realized nothing could be done on that side. My husband told him that I was in no way to blame but that he didn't love me any more. The bishop then authorized me to go home to my parents, which I have done. I have always behaved as the law of God directs, but I am still young and exposed to many temptations. Like other women in like circumstances, I don't know how long I can hold out. We are human and there is a limit to our strength.

"This is my question. Has the Church, who is our mother, forgotten all about us? Is there no way for her to help us? We are human. What we want is a man to protect and love us, a man we can love, a husband to give us children. I live with my parents, but they are getting on in years and nobody lives for ever. When they go, I will be exposed—as other women are—to

---

[12] See, for example, Häring's discussion of "Pastoral care of divorced persons who have remarried," in *Marriage in the Modern World* (Westminster, Md.: The Newman Press, 1965), p. 364.

many dangers. For the love of God, Bishop, keep on fighting. Don't stop until the Church comes up with some solution for special and exceptional cases like ours, where it is possible to prove total desertion and adultery by the other party. There are so many abandoned women, and people think that we are loose livers and that our children are illegitimate. Help us, please."

Most divorced women remarry. On the basis of the survey mentioned earlier, Goode says that 94 per cent of women who divorce by the age of 30 marry again.[13] In countries which do not permit divorce, the strong moral and religious pressures lower the proportion of illicit unions, especially among conservative groups. In all such cases, the most painful factor from the religious viewpoint is the separation from the religious community, which excludes the divorced and remarried, even when they lead an exemplary family life and profess deep religious beliefs. This letter from France is typical of many in Archbishop Zoghby's possession.

"I was only 19 when I began to go with a young man who lived nearby. My parents disliked him and tried to break it up, but we loved each other with a pure and sincere love. My mother was very strongwilled, and when France was liberated in 1944, she made me write him a letter to end our relationship, and she then introduced me to a lawyer from the South.

"I had been raised in a Catholic family, in which the children were taught to obey without question. I was terrified of my parents' anger, and I lacked the courage to discuss my problems with anyone. I was completely desolate. Because of his economic and social standing, the lawyer had the full backing of my parents. At first he hid from me the fact that he was a Protestant. When I learned about it, I thought I could make it an excuse to break off. He, however, told my mother that he wanted to become a Catholic, and the two of them pushed ahead with the arrangements for the marriage.

"During our short courtship, I always felt fear and apprehension in his presence. I could tell that below the surface all was lies and hypocrisy. On our wedding day I was humiliated. I had

[13] Goode, *op. cit.*, p. 277.

invited a girl friend, and my husband did nothing all day but pay attentions to her. He carried his insult to the point of visiting her the following day in her apartment and staying for a considerable time. Because of such conduct, I became ill, and my fears grew stronger. I found myself even less willing than before to discuss my despair with anyone. Two months passed before the marriage was consummated.

"Fifteen months after this unhappy marriage, we had a child. Far from strengthening our very tenuous bonds, however, this became the excuse for leaving mother and son alone in the house. I could not escape being aware of my husband's misconduct. Within three years, I had a nervous breakdown, a development which gave my husband the opportunity to get a divorce. I had to return to my parents, with my son. Since then I have lived alone for 15 years, working usually at night to educate the child. Suffering and tears have been my constant companions, but I have continued to struggle. In such circumstances, the life of a Christian woman is harsh. I have known periods of anguish and total despair.

"A few years ago I met a young man who was very good to us and who has been of great help to my son. Our friendship grew gradually into a deep feeling of mutual confidence. He has been my one support in my worst moments. My spiritual director has been a good father to me. I love and respect him. On his advice, I applied for a declaration of nullity. The proceedings dragged on for three years, and in the end I was turned down for lack of proof. My son, now aged 17, has also suffered enormously because of my situation. He advised me to marry the young man who had become my closest companion. Others whose views I respected said the same thing. It took me a long time to make up my mind, but we were married a week ago, and although it was only a civil ceremony, in our hearts we asked God to bless our union.

"Two days after our marriage, the radio notified us that your Excellency at the Council had asked the Western Church, which should give an example of love and charity, to adopt the more humane regulations of the Eastern Church in the case of the spouse who has been unjustly abandoned. My husband and I are praying to God and asking the intercession of Our Lady that the Church will give consideration to its children who find themselves in this situation, so that we will no longer feel rejected but experience the love of God as a father who comforts his children in the hour of their grief.

"We are unable to receive Christ, no matter how intensely we want to do so. In our unhappy situation, we ask for all Christians the understanding and prayers of the entire Council."

The next two letters dwell on the situation of faithful Catholics who have intimate relations with a divorced or separated person, though prevented by social conventions or religious belief from formalizing the relationship by means of a civil marriage. When such cases are included, the total number of those affected by the present strict rules of canon law increases considerably.

The first is from Switzerland. "My problem is this. I am unmarried, a practicing Catholic, and for seven years the girl friend of a man who was married but finally abandoned by his wife after she already had a number of adventures. First of all, she had a son by him. Then she deceived him by going out with another man. Later, while they still lived together, she became pregnant, though definitely not by her husband. Her next step was to take off and marry her lover in a civil ceremony. They now have still another child and continue to live together.

"The unfortunate first husband was left with his mother and his son. He realized that there was no possibility of a reconciliation. In due course, I became acquainted with him, and we were attracted to each other. Like me, he is a Catholic, and he did not want to break the law of the Church. So we kept on waiting, always hoping that the Church would do something for the innocent spouse. As you can understand, we put all our trust in the Council, and when we learned about your intervention on September 23, we were convinced that finally a solution of our delicate problems was at hand. Subsequently, to our unspeakable distress, the newspapers told us that your view was challenged, and that the Council would do absolutely nothing to help us. . . ."

The other letter is from Italy. "For the longest time, I weep in bed every night. When I close my eyes, I hope I will never open them again. If only I could lie absolutely still without thinking, so that on awakening in the morning I would not have to start the suffering, the thinking and the torment all over again! I am frightened at each new day as it unfolds before me, frightened that something or someone will separate me from the man I love, because my way of life is disgraceful and full of deceit.

"Why, why should life be so hard on one who has already suffered, on one who wants to build a new home, to raise a family, to live in true and lasting contentment? Such are the questions I ask myself every day, and they float away into the void, hanging like unanswered prayers. I have knocked at many doors. I have appealed to many people for help. I have prayed more than I thought possible. All has been in vain. Simply nothing. Not even a hope, not even a tenuous self-deception to help me to stay alive and look forward to a better tomorrow. 'You must leave him,' they tell me. 'You must act as though he had never entered your life.' I ask you, Archbishop Zoghby, is that just? He is alone. He is sad. He is unfortunate and sick with tuberculosis. He is bitter and disenchanted. He has no purpose in life to take him out of himself and make him smile here below. Yet they tell me to leave him, to walk out and drop him back into the void of his loneliness. That is something I cannot do. What is more, I believe with all my heart that the Lord who is good and merciful would not want me to do it. God taught me to love the weak, to love my neighbor as myself. God taught me to be generous, to love the afflicted, the sick, the needy.

"Allessandro needs me, Archbishop Zoghby. This you must believe. He needs affection to give him courage, a friendly smile to light his path, a good word to console him. Our Lord left his whole flock to go after a single sheep that needed him. By this sublime act of love and generosity, he taught us to help those who feel lost, useless and alone, giving our own lives to save them. All I want is one thing, to be at his side to help him forget, to be at his side to return the smile and the joy in his heart, to be at his side to create with him a new family."

II. DOCTRINAL GROUNDS

The victims of the Church law which says marriage cannot be dissolved ask themselves what is the reason for such institutional intransigence. They compare their personal experience with what the Scripture says and what preachers proclaim in the pulpit, and they come to doctrinal conclusions which often show deep perception and sound Christian and human instincts. The student who attempts a scientific survey of the matter can only be deeply impressed by the ability to cut through to the essentials shown by those with direct and personal experience. Christ's statement that "the spirit breathes where he will" quickly takes on for him a deeper meaning.

The Italian weekly ABC received 31,293 answers from all over the country to a survey it made in 1965 and 1966. The most common reasons given in favor of divorce were the following:

1. Divorce completes individual freedom.

2. Divorce represents the need to resolve in a just way the breakdown of a marriage.

3. "Separation" without the possibility of divorce is a hypocritical and contradictory institution. It dismembers the family without providing the possibility of founding a new one.

4. Divorce is the logical consequence of an irreparable break.

5. Life in common is meaningless unless it is based on mutual love and esteem.

6. Unions maintained by force can lead to tragedy.

7. There has to be a way to remake one's life after a youthful mistake.

8. Others must adapt themselves to the practice of more advanced countries.

9. It is important to get children out of an atmosphere of tension and hate.

10. Extreme cases provide indisputable evidence that divorce is to be admitted in principle.[14]

This summary is included here simply as background infor-

[14] Fortuna-Jorio-Pandini, p. 27.

mation and as an indication of how people are thinking in one of the few countries in the world which does not admit civil divorce.

When we turn to strictly religious motivations, the Zoghby correspondence provides reasons based principally on a reflection on the divine justice and mercy. When reading these letters, one would think that the writers were familiar with the statement of St. Thomas Aquinas that "mercy is a kind of fulness of justice."[15]

Here are some of the thoughts raised by the severity of the Church law in the minds of four of those affected by it. The first is from Spain. "In the light of the already stated facts and recalling the reason for our Lord's coming on earth, not only to offer his precious life as a holocaust for those thirsting after justice, but also to make us understand by his suffering greater than death and his example of love, charity, goodness and understanding that we should love one another, we have to face the fact that we are still destroying each other, if not materially at least morally, so that we are really dead while still alive.

"How many examples of wisdom Christ gave us! Take the case of Mary Magdalene. Without criticizing the justice of men, he prevented the crowd from carrying out its intention of stoning one they considered a woman of loose life simply by saying that the one who was sinless should cast the first stone. He restored the dead to life. He made the paraiyzed walk. He directed Peter to build a Church to be a source of life and love. He inspired the gospels as a guide for men of good will and not as a harsh code of laws to condemn humans to banishment from his soul and heart.

"He established his Church so that it would open wide its doors to welcome all thirsting for justice, and not to close them against those who appeal to the divine justice to allow them what God has ordained for every human being, no matter how poor and miserable."

The next is from Italy. "Your most human and consequently most Christian proposal will of course be rejected by the hier-

---

[15] St. Thomas Aquinas, *Summa theologiae*, I, q. 21, a. 3, ad 2.

archical 'superiors' (superiors only in terms of their position) for the usual and oft-repeated reasons, although those reasons most definitely do not reflect in any way the infinite goodness and justice of our Lord."

A French correspondent refuses to abandon hope. "Can the shepherd who loves and watches over his flock voluntarily surrender one of his sheep to the wolf? Never. He defends it with every means at his disposal. Will he leave a sick sheep behind without having used all his skills to cure it? On the contrary, he stays beside it as long as any prospect of a cure remains, hoping that it will soon be able to take its place again in the midst of the flock which goes forward peacefully in the love of its Lord, confident that it is constantly being watched over. Is it right for us, therefore, to abandon that sheep which the wolf grabbed one day in his cowardly fashion and left wounded? Do you think that God will reproach the one who helped and tended that injured sheep, making together their way towards the Lord? I am convinced he will not. What would be the purpose of a religion, if it forbids those who know and love God as best they can, and who believe in Christ, to follow the example of his love and clemency, and to give help in such catastrophic circumstances to those who suffer through no fault of their own? If that is so, I ask both you and myself what can I hope for, what can I do, what can I think.

"I have confidence in God, and I have full confidence in you who represent him with so much piety. I trust you can find a solution, in harmony with our holy Church, to enable us to hope again and to rebuild what vice had destroyed, thus giving us the most precious stone, the foundation stone in the new building which we two shall raise for the love of God, so that this new home will last for ever. . . ."

Another Spaniard, faithful but distressed, adds his comment. "My dear Father. I no longer know if the God in whom I believe still exists, or if other people have a different God. I believe in the God who said that we should love each other, who told us never to think of the evil others had done us but only in the good that we ourselves had left undone. Never close your mind in on your reasons for self-justification, but be open to the arguments in favor of the position of others. Think of the beauty of love and the salvation of your soul. Bitterness and hatred are the cancer of petty minds. Do not despond when things go against you, but lift your head to the Lord and he will help you."

Theologians are starting to ask what is left in a marriage once mutual love is gone. "When a man and a woman find it impossible to continue to live the meaning of the sacrament," writes Father Christian Duquoc, O.P., "the institution has lost all meaning for them. All that remains is social or religious constraint. . . . Many are the cases in which the initial encounter never took place."[16] Starting from this principle, Father Duquoc draws some very reasonable conclusions which will be set out in the last chapter. Here it is proper to note that other theologians still insist on talking about "a community of salvation," even in the case of marriages so utterly destroyed that no hope of reconciliation survives. Thus, Father Bernard Häring, although normally found in the pastorally progressive camp, asserts that "the community of salvation established by the sacrament continues."[17]

Here is the view of a separated spouse on this aspect of the marriage bond. The writer, an Italian, expresses both his faith and his common sense. "If it is certain that man should not part what God has joined, it is no less certain that love is a gift of God, and when that feeling has disappeared through the fault of one or the other, God has already divided those two human beings. The dislike and possible hatred which they now experience for each other is inspired by the devil and prevents their living together. It is both Christian and human to separate them and give them the possibility of finding tranquility, peace and love once more."

When Catholics argue against divorce, they invariably stress the great harm it does to the the social order. Cardinal Dino Staffa, a longtime intransigent of the Roman Curia, is a spokesman for this viewpoint. "Supporters of divorce in Italy argue that the large number of illegitimate unions makes it proper, if

---

[16] Christian Duquoc, *Le Mariage* (Tournai: Mame, 1967), p. 179.
[17] Bernard Häring, *Le chretien et le mariage* (Paris, 1965), p. 114.

not obligatory, for the state to introduce divorce and bring happiness to these unhappy people. This is like claiming that the great number of thefts, robberies and murders indicates a need to change our attitude towards the offenders, opening the jail gates and abolishing the penalties for such crimes. It is an absurdity in the moral order, even prior to that in the legal order, to damage one of the axes of social life for the happiness of some people, particularly when they are the guilty ones. The state should keep citizens on a high moral level and not make it easy for them to fall."[18]

The point of view of those affected, as expressed in the following letter from Italy, is quite different. "After a full study of the issues, I have reached the definite conclusion that such a viewpoint is wrong and influenced by external motives. I have consequently separated myself openly from the Church and the sacraments, and I have drawn closer to the spirit of Jesus who never sought to hurt anyone. At the same time, my love of the truth has driven me to search for the reasons (and assess their value) which have caused the Church to refuse permanently, categorically and absolutely to re-examine this unhappy sector of the laws of Western Christianity. This is of course a reason and a serious one. It is fear or rather an irrational dread (of the consequences). But it is not (in my opinion) sufficient.

"My question is whether divine or human laws can authorize the denial of justice to one who has a right to it, simply out of fear that such charity may be abused by the malice of the modern world, a world which admittedly is ready to invent and fabricate improper motives for separation and to cause even greater suffering than that of the real victims of human weakness and thoughtlessness. When Jesus justified the loving effort for the ox which had fallen into a pit on the Sabbath, and when he urged that the ninety-nine sheep safe in the sheepfold should be left alone while the shepherd went to search for the one that was lost, he had no fear that he would destroy respect for observance of the Sabbath rest (still maintained in our days), nor that the 99 sheep would come to harm by being left alone

[18] "Divorzio né grande né piccolo" in *Concretezza*, Milan, April 15, 1955.

for a while. Could anyone imagine a Jesus without concern for his poor one, satisfied because he had jealously observed the letter of the holy law, or because he had stood faithful guard over his sheepfold?

"In consequence, much as I respect and admire the works of the Church, I have no choice but to oppose its position on this issue, because through fear or misguided prudence it changes the basic meaning and spirit of the gospel, a spirit and meaning which are here an expression of justice. While ready to pardon beyond the point of credibility the inevitable, inescapable, sinful and sorrowful consequences of impossible states of life, the Church is not prepared to do justice. Is the Church's idea perhaps that those whose marriages are in trouble will take another look when they seek the hopelessly sad situation of those who have no solution to their problem? But when did Christ leave people without a solution to their problem?

"I ask, therefore, if such an approach is lawful and beneficial, or if on the contrary one must condemn as unlawful an approach which goes against human nature and Christian principles. If we study the peoples of the East, can we say that the consequences feared by the Catholic Church are verified? What remedies does the Eastern Church offer, or rather, what precautions does it take to ensure that the granting of justice when appropriate is not harmful to others? And taking into account the hesitance of the Catholic Church, what can we do to persuade it to end its inhuman harshness?"

At the Vatican Council, Patriarch Maximos IV Saigh commented ironically on the "bachelor complex" underlying the approach of many of his fellow clerics to the problems of marriage. Others would go further, challenging the competence of a celibate clergy to judge such issues. Such is the viewpoint expressed in this letter from Italy. "To sum up, you priests are the ones technically least qualified to talk about marriage, because you renounced it, 'making yourselves eunuchs.' And since you cannot understand the sorrow of a separation, just as we cannot understand the joy you feel in your solitude, you should stick precisely to what Jesus said, and not employ the word of God to suit your convenience."

Of particular importance is the next testimony, because of its reference to views expressed by Pope John XXIII when he was nuncio to France. It is here published for the first time. "I submitted my case to Msgr. Roncalli when he was nuncio in Paris. He honored me with his friendship, and he used to come from time to time to relax in my place. This, he said to me, 'is one of those unhappy situations which the Church must correct as quickly as possible.' But as far as I can see, the fruit is not yet ripe. . . ."

III. PSYCHOLOGICAL ASPECTS

Two of the major problems of those who are separated and not remarried are the loneliness and the worry of an unbalanced life. The loneliness of the woman is aggravated by social structures which in most countries assume that normal life for a woman involves the notion of "protection." It is considered a virtue in the law to give effective and wide protection to women, even at the cost of limiting their opportunities for personal development and denying them social stability in their own right. The abandoned wife in these circumstances finds herself doubly alone. Her personal loss is constantly emphasized by her social situation.

The following letter describes the situation as seen by three Chilean women. "We are Catholic women, married in Church several years ago and subsequently abandoned—together with our children—by our respective husbands. We were guilty of no misconduct to cause them to leave us. Now they live in bigamy, having forgotten both their children and us completely, and not giving us any material support.

"We are turning to your Excellency, because we learned in the newspapers that the Church is finally going to take account of women like ourselves who have been left alone and without hope. In God's name we ask you not to forget us, but to help us in some way. We are still young and we have the right and the desire to have homes of our own, a father for our children, a husband to shield and protect us, a man who will love us and whom we can love freely and wholeheartedly. We have always lived as God and the Church directed, since we are Catholics, but our strength to endure such a life lessens each day, and temptations are many.

"We know that the Church is concerned today more than ever before with efforts to resolve all the world's problems. Can it be that we are still ignored? Can it be that we will get no kind of help? The Church is a mother, and a mother forgets none of her children. Will this mother not remember us? Will she not stretch out a hand to raise us from this sea of confusion, danger and temptation in which we have been living for so many years? This is why we have the courage to appeal to you with all our hearts to help us. Do not forget us. Please do not join everyone else in abandoning us.

"We want to have a little married happiness, just as does every woman who decides to marry, but we also want to have the blessing of God and to stay in the Church. We want to continue to be women worthy to be called children of God, and only you can help us. We have written several times to the Roman Rota and were told to go to our own bishop, but we have decided to address you instead and look forward to your reply. The Chancery of our diocese has told us they can do nothing for us."

A Frenchwoman offers a similar testimony. "My husband left me when I was ill in the hospital for 18 months, with tuberculosis of the bone, after the birth of our second daughter. That was seven years ago, and since that time I live alone and enjoy good health. If there are happy moments in my life in spite of everything, my two daughters deserve the thanks. But something is lacking to complete my happiness.

"I am thirty, and I need a normal home and someone beside me to support me. I need to be loved. I need to feel that I am not alone always and in all circumstances. I consider this indispensable for the normal development of a mother and necessary for the happiness of the children. I have been fighting alone for seven years and winning my battles. I feel at times that I am falling into an abyss out of which I can never hope to climb. I am on the point of doing something crazy. But at the last moment I see my children before my eyes, and that keeps me from sinking.

"There is also God, whom I love greatly, and in whom I have placed all my confidence. But I tell myself at times that he is a very demanding God. Or should I not rather say that it is the men who are very demanding? Often during all these years I have had time to reflect, and I tell myself that the good God is more understanding than the men, and that he will be forgiving with somebody like me who wants to build a new life. I beg you, Excellency, to tell me what I can do to live normally without losing my peace of mind. . . ."

The trials and imbalance of a life alone, when a person's vocation was to the life of a community in marriage, can become a source of emotional disturbance, or at best, a factor tending to destroy personality. Catholic sociologists are the first to note that statistics indicate a high suicide rate among the divorced.[19] The next four letters can provide a fruitful field of study for psychiatrists and sociologists, and possibly also for novelists and script writers. Unfortunately, all four describe true-life incidents, real dramas enacted by four faithful Catholics under the sunny skies of France.

"I have set out to the best of my ability my situation, my fears and my hopes. I should like to believe that these few pages, written with full awarenss in the presence of God, can concretely help you to understand (if you do not already do so) the void in which we live, especially when one of us goes to the parish priest for advice and gets always the same answer: 'You are wasting your time and mine.' On such occasions, one's faith seems to disappear, and all that is left is a question: where is the Church's clemency; where is the love of God they are forever preaching? I am sure our Lord cannot approve such illogicalities. What strength we need on such occasions, after we have tried everything, when such a wave prevents us from reaching the shore only a few yards away! How many have thrown themselves into this abyss for lack of a kind hand to hold them back!

[19] In *Perché no il divorzio* (Milan, 1963, p. 79), Armando Guidetti, S.J., claims that divorced persons provide a substantial part of the statistics on suicides, delinquency, mental illnesses and prostitution. Bernard Häring agrees (*Marriage in the Modern World*, p. 364). See also the already mentioned comment of the French bishops in *La Documentation Catholique*, 64, col. 1713.

By this path many Christians have strayed from God's road. As for me, I am determined to fight wind and tide as long as my strength endures. You have restored our hope enormously, so that we can step with more assurance on the road which seems to slide away from under our feet. Believe me when I tell you that I pray with all my soul for a great light to illuminate the darkness in which we are groping."

Next comes the testimony of a war veteran. "I had the misfortune to be called up in 1939, and when I got back in 1946, I found my home empty. My wife had gone back to her parents and wanted nothing more to do with me. Given my vocation to a family life, it would be superfluous to describe my shock or to tell you how deeply I suffered by reason of this abandonment. I make my livelihood in a technical profession, and I must have a person to take care of my home. But I have failed to find a loyal servant. Every woman who comes tries to get a hold on me as soon as she discovers that I live alone, and she soon lets me know that her ambition is to become my wife. As a faithful Catholic, I have always refused, with the consequence that my entire life has been unbalanced from the viewpoint of emotions and affection. I have lived like a shipwrecked man, without a home, without tenderness, without a support.

"This is why I write to beg you to do something for the poor unfortunates who have been abandoned by their spouses without deserving so much unhappiness. With a full knowledge of what is involved, I want to tell you that they lead an absolutely impossible life. Helped by my religious principles, I have done everything in my power to swim against the current. But I want you to know that I have suffered since 1945 an intolerable calvary which I would not wish on my worst enemy. Nobody has a right to ask a young man to live so solitary a life. The Lord himself said that it was not good for man to be alone."

The same sentiments are echoed in the next letter. "Do you really believe, Archbishop, that something will be done in the future to enable the many Christians who like me live in suffering to recover their peace of mind and not fall into despair, hatred of the Church or sin? Because, to speak frankly, I believe there are very few who have the strength to say at every moment of their lives, 'Thy will be done.' A person repeats the phrase and pounds it into his head. But the days go by and the same old problems reappear. Then we are assaulted by temptation and by despair. There is no solution other than the heroism which has been forced on us and to which we are obliged. Despair draws us to seek the most improper solutions, even to the extent of suicide. I know that is cowardice, but the desperate man is no coward."

What it is like to have lived in this void for long years is told by one who has done just that. "I am now 50 and completely alone. I regard my life as meaningless, because I cannot give anything to anyone. I have a fierce job which will burn me out quickly. It is my way to stay sane."

Pietro Germi brought to the screen the incoherence of the Italian legislation on marriage. "Divorce, Italian Style" was understood outside Italy as a caricature, a fictional creation with only a slight basis in reality. But Italians and those who have lived in Italy know full well that even what was invented in that film was true to life. Here is a letter to show just how true.

"This morning I read in ABC your thoughtful intervention at the Council in favor of divorce in Italy. I can speak for thousands who, like me, are condemned by the Church to suffer the penalty of a mistaken marriage. For 12 years I have been separated from my wife. During all that time we have never seen each other. And for 12 years I have lived alone with my sad thoughts. The only reason for all this is that it was my misfortune to have been born in Italy. A Catholic marriage has bound me for the past 12 years, forcing me to do penance like a condemned man for a crime I did not commit. My religion went near to making me an assassin. If I had committed a crime of honor 12 years ago, I would now 12 years later be able to start a new life. But the Church has no right to teach people to commit such crimes. As a Christian, I am unable to stain my faith with blood, even if I lost my faith in God and his ministers 12 years ago. I was married in 1946. Six months later, my wife deceived me, because she already had a 7-year-old girl at school. All I could get was a legal separation, but what good is it to be separated and yet remain tied together for life? Who can look forward with joy to the death of one or the other?"

IV. THE CHILDREN

One of the strongest arguments of the defenders of the absolute indissolubility of marriage is the very serious harm suffered by the children of divorced parents. Cardinal Dino Staffa waxes eloquent on this subject, too. "The children become orphans while their parents are still alive. They are sacrificed to the violent passions of the father and mother who may give them other brothers and sisters they can no longer love."[20]

The viewpoint thus expressed is patently subjective. First of all, in very many divorces there are no children. Glick's survey in the United States showed that half of all the marriages which ended in divorce in 1950 were childless.[21] According to Häring, statistical studies show that marriages without children or with only one child are more threatened by divorce. "It follows from Thomas's statistical analysis that 35.3 per cent of those who sought to separate had no children, and that another 27.3 per cent had only one child. Germany's divorce statistics show even higher percentages. Childless marriages constituted 38 per cent of divorces, and there was only one child in another 33 per cent."[22]

In addition, it happens very frequently that the real harm to the children comes from inability to get a divorce. To destroy a family is certainly undesirable, but it is far worse to be unable to create a new home for the children. Two letters express this point very forcibly, as it actually occurs.

The first is from France. "Christ's life and death conferred on the Church not only the message of truth and light, *but also the authority to hold back the divine graces.* But the Church neglects these graces when it systematically denies the least part of the sacraments, the right to be a godparent, the right to

[20] In article cited in note 19, above.
[21] Glick, *op. cit.*, p. 140. The figures cover 22 states.
[22] Häring, *Marriage in the Modern World*, p. 353. The citation from John L. Thomas is from *Catholic Viewpoint on Marriage and the Family* (New York: Doubleday–Image, 1965).

religious burial, and even makes our children—the innocent victims—feel the consequences of its intransigence. When it operates
in this way, the Church erects a screen between our tortured
souls and God."

The other is from Italy. "I am a father and am 47 years old.
I am an unfortunate man and my heart is full of sorrow, because
the world and the laws made by men prevent me from regularizing the situation of my three beloved children, for no cause
except that they were born out of wedlock. Yet at the same
time, the children my lawful wife bears to various other men
can be registered with my name. Only the very rich can afford
the legal costs involved in repudiating paternity of such children, and we who barely make enough to live have to suffer
the indignity. Moreover, when I die, the woman who betrayed
me and those registered as my lawful children although I am not
their father will get whatever I leave, while my true children—
blood of my blood—will have nothing but the shameful mark
of N.N. (no name)."

V. Imposed Celibacy

The law of the indissolubility of marriage becomes at times
one of imposed celibacy. This subject will be discussed at some
length in the final chapter. It suffices here to cite the words of
those involved as a striking refutation of the theory of "a vocation to celibacy as a result of abandonment."[23]

First, a comment from Spain. "I went to my pastor, to my
bishop, and to canon lawyers, and always I got the same answer.
'No, you cannot marry again.' I had never made a vow of
chasity, nor had I the wherewithal to become a saint overnight.
. . . For thirty long years I have borne my cross without any
other union that would have been unlawful, but always fighting
with the help of my firm faith against that *no* which in the
depth of my conscience always came out as a *yes*. If I had the
right to have a wife, if I had the right to a good and proper
Christian home, I ought not to be the victim because of my

---

[23] As developed, for example, by Cardinal Charles Journet in "Le
Mariage indissoluble" in *Nova et Vetera*, 1966, No. 1 (reprinted in *La
Documentation Catholique*, 63, col. 1083).

strong Catholic convictions while she continued on her merry way as a publicly known and certified libertine."

Then this from an Italian woman. "Why, dear brother, why was I singled out for a fate of such loneliness? I was born to be a wife and mother, to love and live my life as a woman fully but honestly. I was not bad, and there was no reason why I should be punished like this. I ask myself why again and again, yet never get an answer. It is not the whole truth to say that God sends the evil so that he can later send a reward. Indeed no, because God is love, and love can be won only by giving love. There is no need to cause suffering in order to recompense.

"Life has been bitter for me. From early childhood I have had to pay may contribution to sorrow merely for having been born. I never asked to be born. Why then cause me so much suffering? If God knew I would have to suffer so much, why did he bring me into the world? Yes indeed, bishop. There are many questions to which I find no answer. And I suffer intensely."

Next, a letter from an Italian man. "What is my problem? I am legally separated from my wife by court order, and I am in love with a young girl. My wife walked out on me only a few months after we were married, leaving me from that day in a deep depression. Actually she started going out frequently, leaving everything in disorder, within a few days of our marriage. And now it is unjust to have to continue several years later to pay for something—for which I was not to blame in the first instance—when I have already done penance and am still doing penance. Like so many others, I took my grief and despair to the pastor, to the coadjutor, to the bishop. With their many fine words, they all said the same thing. 'You must resign yourself to living alone. You must observe continence. You must seek comfort in prayer.'

"But that—as you properly point out—presupposes the possession of virtue in a heroic degree, a rare faith, or an unusual temperament. Most do not resign themselves. Instead, they enter into an unlawful union—as we plan to do—so as not to sink into despair in their acute loneliness, in their sad awareness that they have lost what is most important in life, the intimacy of a family."

The next letter is from France. "I was married in 1948 and had three children, Richard, Louis, and Pierrette, now aged respectively 16, 13, and 8. My husband left me and never came back. He has broken the marriage contract. I no longer have any confidence in him. In my heart it is as if he had actually died. That was five years ago, and I have since devoted my life to my children. I have endured poverty, humiliations and illnesses. I have lived hours of suffering and sadness. There was no reason why my children should suffer. It was my job to love them and make them happy. Life was difficult from one day to the next. I was carrying the grave responsibility of the upbringing and education of my children. . . . I have followed the advice of a priest who encouraged me to learn how to forget, to pardon, to give up everything, loving Jesus Christ and abandoning myself to him. The Lord has loaded me down with graces. He has given me strength, peace and joy. We are happy and fortunate, in spite of our material poverty.

"Nearly a year ago, however, something new happened. I met a marvellous man, one with wonderful qualities, an ideal man. This was at a time when I had given up all thought of ever again loving or being loved. This friendship developed into a relationship of extraordinary mutual esteem, a spiritual and supernatural union. It is based entirely on God. He is love. He knows our love, our intentions, our desires, our promises. The Lord directed him to me. We are God's instruments. What should we do? Should we give up our union? That would be impossible. Have we not the right to be happy? With all our hearts we want the blessing of the Church."

Finally, a note from Mexico. "Dear Archbishop, the Holy Spirit has enlightened you, and it is God's will that many souls will be saved if your proposal is approved. It will prevent many assassinations and many suicides. People will no longer avoid being married in the Church, and the spouses who are deceived will not have to curse the Church, because they will have a prospect of remaking their lives and their homes. God has chosen you to save and help all the deceived spouses who find themselves in the same bitter situation as I do."

VI. Religious Life of the Divorced

Opponents of divorce, especially if they are members of the class of ecclesiastical officialdom, usually pinpoint "the violent passions" of the spouses as the cause of breakdown and remarriage. In their view, divorce and remarriage are always the fruit of the continuing attraction to evil which infects the human condition.

Following the same line of thought, it is standard practice to overlook the religious sentiments of divorced Catholics, assuming that such sentiments are nonexistent. If a faithful Catholic disobeys the Church on a point of such gravity, it seems logical to conclude that he lacks authentic faith and the desire to lead a religious life. The divorced person who remarries is excluded from the sacraments for an unlimited period of time,[24] and it is only recently that the initiative and good sense of priests in many countries have begun to search for a way to ease this situation. They are doing this, because their pastoral experience has established that very many divorced and remarried Catholics profess a sincere faith and desire vehemently to lead a religious life. It may well be that suffering and disenchantment have crystallized their religious sense. What is clear is that for many the element in their situation that causes the greatest distress is their rejection by the Church and their exclusion from the sacraments. And in spite of all the lack of understanding, the strong faith of many survives, so that they manage to retain their confidence in a Church which closes its doors to them and turns its back.

Such is the message of a correspondent from the United States. "Your plea for more leniency for divorced Catholics who have remarried gives hope to thousands of excommunicated Catholics who also want so much to return to the sacraments and are in such a bind with family ties and family problems they cannot bring themselves to the desertion of a second spouse, as now necessary, to return to the church.

"These people are facing a gamble of outliving the first or second partner of the marriages, or hoping to be a death-bed

---

[24] Canon 2356 as modified by the 1966 instruction *Matrimonii sacramentum*. See below, p. 189.

Catholic. These people should be given as much consideration to return to the church as the fallen-away Protestants, I would think. . . . Enlist the aid of American churchmen, as they too know the great problem here in America. I'll be praying for your continued fight and eventual success for some sort of reprieve to get these people (I am one) back to the sacraments, as every day and year is a continued fear of death outside the church, and still unable to muster the cruelty it woud take to cut out from the second marriage. I am nervous as I write this letter and only hope you can read it. I have tried for twenty years to end the second marriage and return to the church, but cannot bring myself to think of myself first."

Similar sentiments are expressed in this letter from Italy. "I speak from my own unhappy experience. Because of the indissolubility of marriage, I have lived an entire lifetime (35 of my 55 years) of sorrow, of continual mortifications and utter misery. How much sorrow has been spread around in those long years! The man who cannot remarry has no choice but to take and discard his victims along the way, nor can the woman establish a new home or join an honorable man lawfully. It is very sad indeed that no thought is given to finding a remedy for so much moral evil. Those affected by it are also the children of God. Their lot is a most unhappy one, and all they have to look forward to is the freedom death will bring. Freedom through death, do I say? But if it is their misfortune that death should come while two who love and treasure each other are living under the same roof, will the result be freedom? Or, because they cannot have the consolation of the holy sacrament, will they have to suffer after death, too?"

As part of this study, it becomes necessary to formulate the religious values enshrined in a marriage between Christians contracted outside the Church. Biblical sources offer little guidance, and the early Fathers—because of their prejudices against "the life of the flesh"—were no more than marginally interested. According to the strict modern Catholic teaching, such a union is totally devoid of religious values for the simple reason that it constitutes a state of sin. Religious phenomenology, nevertheless, tells a very different story. Many Catholics joined in canonically invalid marriages exhibit in these unions the highest level of Christian behavior, making it impossible to assert that the parties are not in the grace of God. The manner and nature of this divine benevolence are a matter of theological speculation. The fact is supported by these two letters, both from French-speaking countries, written by Catholics who entered a non-canonical marriage after one of the spouses was abandoned and divorced.

"Most reverend Council Fathers. With deep respect and immense confidence, we dare to present our request. The Lord has guided us to love. He who is love has enabled us to penetrate the depths of love. My feelings for Dorothy and her feelings for me were born under the sign of charity without any such intention on our part. Our love for each other has always developed in union with love of Christ. It is so deep and broad that words scarcely suffice to give the least understanding of what it means. We live in a total giving of each other, overflowing with dialogue, understanding, respect, confidence and loyalty. It is a complete union of our hearts and spirits under the loving gaze of our Lord.

"We ask the Lord and you, reverend Fathers, for the grace to live this communion of life more fully and intensely in holy marriage, the encounter of love and prelude to eternal happiness. We ask you not to permit the destruction of our mental and moral selves by forcing us to live half a life. The Lord has allowed us to hope in his great goodness and to believe in his infinite mercy. We ask you to hear our petition and not betray our hope and confidence in the Lord and in your decisions. . . ."

The other letter was similarly written in the name of the two parties. "At Mass every Sunday and twice during the week, Archbishop, we join in asking the Lord to turn his gaze to you, to show you his face and give you his peace and blessing. We are under a harsh test and we cannot withstand it by ourselves. After each storm we feel stronger and start out afresh. Our love grows constantly deeper, and our confidence in the Lord expands. He has given us the grace to abandon ourselves to him. We want him to be our guide and pastor, because then we shall want nothing. In spite of the sorrow of many moments, he has always given us his peace and joy. We need him more than we can describe. We want our love to abide in him, so that this will be a sacred union lasting forever, for all eternity. . . ."

In some cases the ecclesiastical penalties can lay claim to the bitter victory of successfully imposing the situation they seek to establish. Such is the message of this letter from the United States.

"My wife deserted and divorced me. This state has prevented me from marrying and raising a family in the Catholic faith. I hesitate because I do not wish to lose the sacraments by marrying. But my status is in the middle of the road and I am helpless. At this time I would like to humbly request you to do all in your power to get a dispensation or a release for people in my situation. God bless you for realizing this course of action, which is sorely being overlooked. It definitely is a cross to carry for people in my situation. Here is hoping your colleagues, the eminent cardinals and bishops, do also realize the importance of this problem."

But alongside the "silent community" of those who have been doubly abandoned is to be found the legion of those who have lost all confidence in the Church and end up by abandoning the faith. The fact is that churchmen have very little to offer to the member of the faithful who has the misfortune to be abandoned without fault. Not only do they have little, they really have nothing. As a rule, the spouse with a problem is channeled through the labyrinth of ecclesiastical courts, and his religious vitality is steadly dissipated through contact with the cold remoteness of the canons. Here are two cases, both from France, in which the faith has simply been lost.

"My son had just married when the war began. Having trained in the 1938 draft, he was recalled to active service in March, 1939. He was taken prisoner soon afterwards and spent five years in a concentration camp. During that time, his wife went to live with another young man, and they had a daughter. My son, on his return, wanted her back. He even offered to take the girl and register her as his own child. His wife would not agree, claiming that the child would always come between them. We made some discreet enquiries and established that she was in fact living with another man.

"I need not describe for you, Archbishop, the depth of my son's disillusionment and discouragement. Finally, however, he recovered and decided to remarry. They now have an 8-year-old boy and are happy. But my son has lost the faith and propagates his ideas wherever he goes. Nor should you think, Archbishop, that his is an isolated instance. This problem has to be studied seriously in order to ease the rigorous rules introduced by the Church in the first centuries. Christ himself would be more understanding in such circumstances."

The next letter, also from a mother, tells how her daughter was affected. "She held out against the divorce for three years but had finally to regularize her situation through the courts. Being very young, she feels deeply the need for affection and motherhood, so that she is disconsolate in her loneliness. What can be done? We tried to get an annulment, but the difficulties raised and the unwillingness to cooperate which we experienced forced us to abandon the effort.

"We always were devout in the exercise of our faith. But when my daughter found herself rejected by the Church, she gave up all religious practice and has lost the faith. I have tried to hold on to it, but deep inside I have suffered a dreadful shock, and this extreme intransigence of the Church has caused my confidence to collapse like a house of cards. I believed that to obey the precepts of the Church was to follow God blindly. Now I know these are two quite different things. I am, of course, under no illusion. I know it is going to take the Church many years to recognize that it is only elementary justice to permit an innocent abandoned spouse to start life afresh. . . ."

In Italy, religious issues always assume political overtones, and divorce is no exception. Here is a testimony to illustrate that situation.

"I belong to the category of those unhappily abandoned by their spouse. After a year of marriage, my wife walked out, leaving a baby boy who is now ten years old. He has never known his mother and has grown up entirely isolated from the family. I ask myself constantly why I have to put up with this sad life, when I should be in a position to work things out so as to have a proper home and my own family group. I tell you sincerely and clearly that I am anticommunist. But when we have elections, my parents, my sisters and I all vote as a bloc for the Communists, because theirs is the only party that holds out for us any possibility of divorce.

"What I want is to live like the people next door, a modest and well-behaved life, but I lack a mate and by myself I seem an incomplete and useless person. I will even tell you that I have become anticlerical, simply because I regard the clergy as my worst enemy as far as understanding and correcting our unhappy situation is concerned. Often at night, especially after my wife left me, I used to ask myself if God existed. How could God authorize such torments? Even admitting that there may be some unfortunates lacking a sense of dignity and love for their children, it is still inhuman to leave honorable people in agony for their entire lives. I always ask myself if it is just to wound the innocent in the same way as the guilty, because that is like imposing the same punishment on the robber and on his victim. And I also often ask myself how many gods are there in the world, when I recall that Catholic countries like France, Germany and others permit divorce, while false shame excludes it in Italy, Spain and Portugal. I am not suggesting that the guilty be granted divorces, since they already know what to expect when they commit treason, but only those deceived by reason of their own excessive generosity."

VII. Can Nothing Be Done?

Those involved have formulated the issues. Their testimony makes it impossible to deny further that sincere and believing Christians exist whose social, moral and religious condition is harmed by a canon law which the Catholic Church alone among Christian denominations maintains. The essence of their message can be formulated in a question and a request. The question is whether the Church can change its discipline on the indissolubility of marriage. The request is that the Church come effectively to the help of innocent abandoned spouses. What remains to be done is to provide materials for study and reflection so that the question can be properly answered. But even if this work does not achieve its purpose, even if it fails to convince those who hold in their hands the instruments of change and renewal, the problem will continue to exist, and it will be necessary to go on searching seriously for an answer. The presence within the community of the Church of thousands of faithful children who do not find there the word of salvation constitutes a real challenge for a Church which should guarantee God's grace to all men in all circumstances.

CHAPTER 3

Scriptural Law and Standards

This chapter will study various scriptural passages dealing with marriage, and especially those referring to divorce. Old Testament quotations will be given with a minimum of commentary, and the major stress will be on the New Testament exchange between Jesus and the Pharisees on the right of repudiation. This is the most important single text of Scripture, because it polarizes all the interpretations of the gospel teaching on marriage and divorce. It is important, at the same time, to distinguish between what it actually says and the way it is understood in the various traditions. What is most important to understand about it is that it is capable of various interpretations. In consequence, it is of little help to the supporters of any of the conflicting doctrinal positions.

I. The Old Testament

Marriage makes husband and wife a single person. When the Pharisees try to provoke Jesus by citing the prescriptions of the law and showing the difficulties they create, his answer is to send them back to the foundation of the law, the Genesis story of the creation of man and woman. "So God created man in his own image, in the image of God he created him; male and female he created them (Gen 1:27).[1] . . . Then the man said, 'This at last is bone of my bones and flesh of my flesh; she shall be called Woman, because she was taken out of Man.' Therefore

[1] This passage belongs to the so-called priestly document in which its story of the Creation begins at 1:1 and runs to 2:4.

a man leaves his father and his mother and cleaves to his wife, and they become one flesh" (Gen 2:23–24).[2]

The phrase translated as "cleave to" literally means to stick to or to tie oneself to, a graphic evocation of the union of the sexes. The effect of this union, nevertheless, is not exclusively bodily. Rather, it fuses husband and wife into the community of a single person. As used in the Bible, the word *flesh* means a person.[3] According to Genesis, therefore, the union of husband and wife in marriage is so close as actually to transcend them and turn them into something new, a single personality formed by their fusion. As Jesus would express it, "they are no longer two" (Mk 10:8). The so-called "priestly account" in Genesis offers an almost metaphysical view of this union by associating it with the image of God (Gen 1:27).

II. UNDER THE LAW

"When a man takes a wife and marries her, if then she finds no favor in his eyes because he has found some indecency in her, and he writes her a bill of divorce and puts it in her hand and sends her out of his house, and she departs out of his house, and if she goes and becomes another man's wife, and the latter husband dislikes her and writes her a bill of divorce and puts it in her hand and sends her out of his house, or if the latter husband dies, who took her to be his wife, then her former husband, who sent her away, may not take her again to be his wife, after she has been defiled; for that is an abomination before the Lord, and you shall not bring guilt upon the land which the Lord your God gives you for an inheritance" (Dt 24:1–4).

It must be noted that this text is not intended to promulgate divorce but to regulate it. The custom of the Jews at that time was to allow the husband to repudiate his wife, leaving them both free to remarry. The phrase *some indecency* translates the Hebrew "erewat dabar," an expression given a variety of meanings from the very earliest rabbinical interpretations.

---

2 This passage belongs to the "Yahwist document," whose story of the Creation begins at 2:5. It is noteworthy that here it is the man who leaves his home to join his wife, a procedure that takes us back to a social situation unknown elsewhere in the Bible.

3 For example, "I will pour out my spirit on all flesh" (Joel 2:28).

The legal action of repudiation is presented within a context of justice and of property rights. The husband is the owner (lord, baal) of his wife. The bill of divorce is the record of his renunciation of his rights, leaving the property available for another owner. Marriage is here considered in strictly legal terms, without the slightest reference to its human and emotional realities. Nevertheless, the Mosaic law softens somewhat the rigidity of previous custom by insisting on the bill of divorce as designed to ensure that the woman will not be left alone without any "protector."

III. Efforts to Rise Above the Law

The legal prescriptions presented in Deuteronomy fall far short of the ideal found in Genesis. The highest minds in Israel were well aware of the contrast, and they called on God's people to return to full observance of the original rule. "So take heed of yourselves, and let none be faithless to the wife of his youth. For I hate divorce, says the Lord the God of Israel" (Mal 2:15–16).

The prophet Hosea offers the example of God who does not abandon Israel in spite of its repeated infidelity. Israel, the wife, becomes a prostitute with different lovers. The Lord threatens to divorce her, but in the end he restores her to his favor. "I will betroth you to me for ever; I will betroth you to me in righteousness and in justice, in steadfast love, and in mercy. I will betroth you to me in faithfulness; and you shall know the Lord" (Hos 2:19–20).

Jeremiah repeats the same theme. "If a man divorces his wife and she goes from him and becomes another man's wife, will he return to her? . . . Return, O faithless children, says the Lord; for I am your master. . . . Surely, as a faithless wife leaves her husband, so have you been faithless to me, O house of Israel" (Jer. 3:1, 14, 20).

Israel, accordingly, knows a higher ideal which urges faithfulness in marriage and discourages use of the right of repudiation granted by the law.[4] God offers himself as an example of patience in bearing with the infidelities of the wife.

---

[4] See also the arguments in favor of the unity of marriage in the so-called Damascus Document of the Qumran sect (4:20 to 5:2). Dupont gives the text in *Mariage et divorce dans l'Evangile*, pp. 25–27.

IV. THE LAW OF THE GOSPEL

The first Christian document to speak of marriage and its possible dissolution is St. Paul's first letter to the Corinthians, written about the year 52. "To the married I give charge, not I but the Lord, that the wife should not separate from her husband (but if she does, let her remain single or else be reconciled to her husband)—and that the husband should not divorce his wife" (1 Cor 7:10–11). "A wife is bound to her husband as long as he lives. If the husband dies, she is free to be married to whom she wishes, only in the Lord" (1 Cor 7:39).[5]

Paul here establishes that as early as about the year 52 a tradition already existed to attribute to Jesus himself certain rules regarding marriage. What he had determined was that the wife should not "separate" from the husband, and that the husband should not "repudiate" the wife. Different words are used for the husband and for the wife. The wife had no right to repudiate her husband, but she could provoke her husband into repudiating her by leaving him and offering him no choice but to write a bill of divorce that would leave her free to remarry. That was what separation meant. According to Jewish law, however, the husband could repudiate his wife.[6] At the same time, it is unlikely that the Corinthians followed Jewish customs, so that these differences of language do not really seem to be very important.

A new limitation is introduced for the woman. She cannot separate, and even if she does leave her husband, she cannot remarry. No similar limitation is laid down for the husband. How is the silence to be interpreted? Most Catholic exegetes hold that the same prohibition applies for the man, and that Paul did not mention it simply to avoid repeating himself. The reason for putting them on the same level is that "if the separated wife re-

---

[5] A parallel text will be found in Rom 7:2.

[6] "Divorce was the act of the man. Though the woman in certain circumstances could claim it, her claim, if the man was obstinately contumacious, could not be enforced. In the last resort, the man could divorce his wife; the woman could not divorce her husband. Thus Rabbinic divorce rests upon inequality. The man has a power which the woman has not" (C. G. Montefiore, *The Synoptic Gospels* [London, 1927], Vol. 1, p. 226). See also "Divorce" in the *Encyclopedia Britannica*.

mains bound, the abandoned husband also remains bound, it being clear that one of the spouses cannot continue to be married
unless the other also is."[7] The conclusion, nevertheless, is not so
obvious as it might seem to be. The history of Christianity is full
of situations in which one spouse has been allowed to remarry
but not the other.[8] Besides, the most distinguished Greek exegetes,
including Origen, have understood the Pauline prohibition as directed only to the wife and not also to the husband.[9] And in
fact, if Paul is read according to legal standards of interpretation,
it must be agreed that he sets up a different rule for husband
and for wife.

It is this writer's view that Christ's command not to remarry
applies also to the husband. To admit this, however, one is forced
to recognize that Paul is not promulgating laws, but simply transmitting the "commands" of Christ which are of quite a different order than those of Moses or the Roman laws. Paul is not
trying to establish a new juridic order. He is transmitting Christian standards for the right use of the things of this world.

Marriage and divorce are things of this world. The Christian
who misuses them is guilty of sin or at least withdraws from the
ideal to which he has been called, but his social and legal status
is not thereby affected in any way whatever. Paul does not tell
the community to treat the husband or wife who remarried after
divorce as guilty of adultery in the legal sense. He simply says
that they have not matched up to Christian standards. Later,
the community will fix a scale of penances for such cases, but
the issue of the "validity" or "invalidity" of the new marital
situation does not arise.

To claim that Paul is drafting a Christian legal code is to make
him say very strange things indeed. For example, he tells the wife
she may not leave her husband, and immediately he introduces
a new "law" directing her to return in case she should leave
him. This makes no sense in legal terms, but it is perfectly intelligible within the moral code of Christian perfection. The

---

[7] Dupont, *Mariage et divorce* . . . , p. 70.
[8] See, for example, the canons of St. Basil as quoted later in this book,
pp. 102ff.
[9] See p. 98.

Gospel rejects both repudiation and separation. But if circumstances make it neccessary, then the community does not condemn the member who is forced in that direction. In such a case, the Christian standard calls on the wife not to remarry, while keeping silent as regards the husband. The community does not regard his remarriage as unlawful, but neither does it approve of it in any way.

This theme will recur later, when an attempt will be made to present a global interpretation of Christ's law concerning marriage, pointing out the differences between this law and the counsels of perfection.

The synoptic tradition has preserved a "saying" of Jesus on the occasion of a discussion of divorce with the Pharisees. The oldest version seems to be that of St. Mark.

"And Pharisees came up and in order to test him asked, 'Is it lawful for a man to divorce his wife?' He answered them, 'What did Moses command you?' They said, 'Moses allowed a man to write a certificate of divorce, and to put her away.' But Jesus said to them, 'For your hardness of heart he wrote you this commandment. But from the beginning of creation, "God made them male and female." "For this reason a man shall leave his father and mother and be joined to his wife, and the two shall become one." So they are no longer two but one. What therefore God has joined together, let no man put asunder.' And in the house the disciples asked him again about this matter. And he said to them, "Whoever divorces his wife and marries another, commits adultery against her; and if she divorces her husband and marries another, she commits adultery" (Mk 10:2-12).

It is obvious that the author has made considerable changes in the tradition as handed down to him in order to make it understandable for non-Jewish readers. The first adjustment concerns the question asked by the Pharisees. In a discussion among Jews, it would simply not make sense for somebody to question the existence of such a well-known law as that granting the right of repudiation. But as we learned earlier from St. Paul, the notion of repudiation was rejected by gentile converts to Christianity. The question accordingly is posed in terms that make it catechetically useful.[10]

Jesus gave a twofold answer. First, he reminded the Pharisees of the integral unity of the divine institution of marriage, as described in Genesis, then pointed out that the Mosaic law represented a step backward because of "the hardness of heart" or faithlessness of men. Next, according to St. Mark, he spelled out his teaching in detail for his disciples only, as was his custom. In this way, he rejected repudiation, branding as adulterers those who made use of it and remarried. Mark's phrase may not repeat what Jesus said word for word. It is unlikely that a Jew would speak of repudiation by the wife. Mark's formula was adapted to the social context of Christians in the Greco-Roman world.[11]

The text of St. Matthew is later, and it introduces some explanatory comments which are extremely interesting for the light they throw on the concerns of Christian communities at the time they were written.

"And Pharisees came up to him and tested him by asking, 'Is it lawful to divorce one's wife for any cause?' He answered, 'Have you not read that he who made them from the beginning made them male and female, and said, "For this reason a man shall leave his father and mother and be joined to his wife, and the two shall become one?" So they are no longer two but one. What therefore God has joined together, let no man put asunder.' They said to him, 'Why then did Moses command one to give a certificate of divorce, and to put her away?' He said to them, 'For your hardness of heart Moses allowed you to divorce your wives, but from the beginning it was not so. And I say to you: whoever divorces his wife, except for unchastity, and marries another, commits adultery.' The disciples said to him, 'If such is the case of a man with his wife, it is not expedient to marry.' But he said to them, 'Not all men can receive this precept, but only those to whom it is given. For there are eunuchs who have been so from birth, and there are eunuchs who have been made eunuchs by men, and there are eunuchs who have made themselves eu-

[10]Dupont, *op. cit.*, pp. 15–16.
[11] See Dupont's explanations, *ibid.*, pp. 61–63.

nuchs for the sake of the kingdom of heaven. He who is able to receive this, let him receive it' " (Mt 19:3–12).

The question is not here the same as that in St. Mark. Repudiation as such is not the issue, but only the reasons for it, and consequently we are being introduced into the central theme of the rabbinical discussions of the phrase *erewat dabar* (Dt 24:1). The controversy over its correct meaning was at its height in the first years of the first century. Hillel the Great was the head of the school which favored a broad interpretation, while his contemporary, Shammai, called for a strict or narrow one.[12] The question of the Pharisees was a request to Jesus to take sides. Specifically, they asked him if he agreed with Hillel that a wife could be repudiated "for any cause."

Jesus answered with an argument from Scripture based on the same Genesis texts as those found in St. Mark. Matthew took his stand on the words of God; Mark, on his acts. For that reason, Matthew attributed to God a phrase from Genesis (2:24) which in the text referred either to Adam or to the writer himself. He contrasted the law of Moses with the original divine law. The Pharisees countered with the Deuteronomy text which regulated repudiation, presenting it as a "command" of Moses. Jesus pointed out that it was merely a "permission," and he immediately appealed to his own authority to overrule Moses, using the accustomed formula of the Sermon on the Mount, "And I say to you. . . ."

It would appear that the statement introduced with this formula was not addressed to the Pharisees but only to the disciples. That is how Mark presented it, and some of the early interpreters agree.[13] This would fit in with the approach commonly used by Jesus of presenting his teaching in two phases, a part for the

---

[12] Both positions are outlined in the Jewish Mishna, Gittin's treatise (9:10) and in the Talmud. Some of the texts can be found in H. L. Strack and P. Billerbeck, *Kommentar zum Neuen Testament aus Talmud und Midrash* (Munich, 1922). Vol. 1, pp. 303–321. Suetonius says that a reaction against divorce abuses occurred in the Roman world in the time of Augustus: "Divortiis modum imposuit" (Suetonius, *Augustus*, 34). The laws of Julia and Papia Poppaea tend to put an end to corrupt practices in the area of marriage, but they do not seem very restrictive as regards divorce.

[13] For example, Clement of Alexandria, in the text cited below at p. 96.

public, and an additional part for his disciples alone.[14] The point has some significance for the general interpretation to be given later.[15]

What is important about the statement made by Jesus to his disciples is that the version given by Matthew includes the famous formula making an exception for cases of adultery. "And I say to you: whoever divorces his wife, except for unchastity, and marries another, commits adultery" (Mt 19:9). Mark merely says: "Whoever divorces his wife and marries another, commits adultery against her" (Mk 10:11).

The just quoted text of Matthew in 19:9 is a parallel of that in 5:32, which reads as follows: "But I say to you that everyone who divorces his wife, except on the ground of unchastity, makes her an adulteress." The meaning of the two phrases is, nevertheless, different. Taken separately and compared with each other, the formulations of Mark and of Matthew do not agree. The absolute exclusion of repudiation by the first is modified by an exception in the second. Some Catholic authors have tried to explain the Greek words used by Matthew in a way that would eliminate the exception, but their attempt carries no conviction.[16] Saint Jerome already gave what is known as the classic solution. He said that the exception referred only to the permission to separate, not to remarriage. According to this interpretation, the intention of Jesus would have been as follows: "The one who divorces his wife (which is allowed only in case of adultery) and marries another (which is always forbidden) commits adultery." This explanation is not accepted by the majority of modern Catholic exegetes,[17] although Jacques Dupont has recently tried to revive it.[18]

Most Orthodox and Protestant writers agree that St. Matthew's

---

[14] Examples are the parable of the sower in Mt 13:1–23, and the question of ritual cleanliness in Mk 7:5–22.

[15] For other explanations of the origin of the *saying* (logion) of Mt 19:9, see Dupont, pp. 38–45.

[16] See the list of these pioneers of the grammar of Catholic Greek in Dupont, *op. cit.*, pp. 96–99.

[17] For example, Vaccari, *Biblica*, 1955, p. 150, and P. Lagrange, 1927, p. 105. *L'Evangile selon St. Matthieu* 3rd Paris ed.

[18] In the excellently documented work already cited several times.

text expresses a true exception to the law of indissolubility. If this is so, Jesus is taking sides with the followers of Rabbi Shammai. Nevertheless, some commentators think that the exception on grounds of adultery is opposed to the teaching of Jesus on marriage taken as a whole.[19] The clause introducing the exception was, according to them, added by the writer in an attempt to accommodate himself to a Christian community of Jewish background and traditions.

It has to be admitted, as a matter of scientific honesty, that no final answer can be given this question in the present state of study and documentation. We cannot know exactly what Jesus taught about divorce. This, nevertheless, does not make unthinkable a global interpretation of the provisions concerning marriage in the New Testament, an interpretation which will help to place the various sayings of Jesus in a proper context, even if it cannot solve all of the problems created by the incomplete way in which they have been passed on to us. Here are some of the points to be taken into account.

1. Jesus addressed his statement to his disciples. This is clearly affirmed by Mark. It is assumed in Matthew 5:32 and can be assumed in Matthew 19:9. The teaching has all the characteristics of an instruction for the Christian community. The words of Jesus give a new meaning to the term *adultery*, a meaning different from that found in Jewish law which knew no such offense as adultery by a husband against his wife.

2. The term *adultery* is not to be taken in a legal sense, as though Jesus was replacing the Jewish law on the subject by his own. Jesus does not tell the community to treat as an adulterer the one who repudiates a spouse and remarries. The intention in very similar to that expressed in the Sermon on the Mount, when Jesus declared: "But I say to you that everyone who looks at a woman lustfully has already committed adultery with her in his heart" (Mt 5:28). The instruction Jesus is giving is designed to establish a moral standard for the disciple, who is told that he should consider the act of repudiation of a spouse to be as immoral as the act of adultery.

[19] Klostermann, Plummer and Allen all note this point in their commentaries on St. Matthew.

3. In Mark's version, the teaching is expressed without legalistic or casuistic concerns. As against those who sought to give the command to repudiate a spouse the backing of the authority of God through his servant Moses, Jesus recalls the true divine institution of marriage. The ideal is set up against the lower standards long tolerated, but without withdrawing the concession. But the disciple of Jesus has undertaken to live at the level of the ideal and must consequently renounce for himself the concession. To repudiate his spouse and remarry would for him be equivalent to adultery. This is a very clearly stated text, and it says that either a husband or a wife who repudiates the other commits adultery. It says nothing about the spouse who is repudiated. In all of this, what is sought is to establish the moral responsibility of the Christian in terms of his commitments to God and to the community, and there is no reference to external legal situations.

4. Matthew's principal concern is to deal with concrete legal situations. The standard set in Mark's text is to treat the question from the viewpoint of the personal responsibility of the disciple who is unable to take the initiative in repudiating his spouse. But real life provides cases in which the separation has in fact taken place, that is to say, cases in which the disciple is the passive victim of an act of repudiation or an equivalent action. The most obvious such case is that of adultery committed by a wife.

Custom condemned the person who continued to live with a wife who had committed adultery, obliging the husband to repudiate her.[20] There was also the possibility that a woman belonging to the Christian community might have been repudiated by her husband. Was she free to remarry? The tradition collected by St. Mark did not answer these two questions. But the rabbinical tradition gave an answer which seemed in line with the teaching of Jesus. In Rabbi Shammai's view, the only reason for repudiating a wife was because of her adultery. Matthew then formulates the question of the justification of repudiating or not repudiating a spouse, in the same way as Mark's formulation concerns repudiation in itself. But Matthew retains the statement

[20] See Mt 1:19: Joseph believes in Mary's innocence yet decides to repudiate her.

of Jesus concerning the rejection of the Mosaic authorization of repudiation, in words similar to those used by Mark. When he gets down to the two concrete cases with which he was concerned, he resolves the case of adultery in line with the teaching of Shammai, but that of the woman who has been repudiated in a restrictive way. In Matthew's view, the husband who repudiates an adulterous wife is not responsible for the repudiation and consequently does not separate what God had joined together.

5. Can the husband who has repudiated his wife because of her adultery remarry? Matthew (19:9) expresses himself ambiguously on the issue, but both the immediate and the remote context create the suspicion that he was trying to avoid a direct answer. The statement of Jesus certainly frees the man who repudiates his wife in those circumstances and remarries from the responsibility for adultery. But what does Jesus think of the new marriage? Matthew's text does not give the answer, but a little later it reproduces the advice given by Jesus with regard to celibacy.[21] The silence of Matthew when it would seem that he should approve the second marriage coincides significantly with the silence of St. Paul when it would seem that he should disapprove of it (1 Cor 7:11), and both silences bring out very clearly the opposition of the Christian community to such marriages, in spite of the fact that they were not considered unlawful.[22]

V. DIVORCE UNDER THE NEW LAW

To state that the law of Christ follows and replaces that of Moses is, to say the least, an inadequate and ambiguous way to describe what happened. The word *law* is used with a different

[21] Clement of Alexandria believed that this counsel was given precisely to the husband who had to repudiate his wife because of adultery. See the text on p. 61, below.

[22] To realize fully what it meant to remain celibate at that time, one must recall that the "lex Julia de maritandis ordinibus" and the "lex Papia Poppaea" enacted by Augustus established that "men aged between 25 and 60 and women between 20 and 50 were obliged to marry, with neither divorce nor widowhood being an adequate excuse for failure to comply." See J. Iglesias, *Instituciones de derecho romano* (Barcelona, published by the author, 1951), Vol. 2, p. 160.

meaning in the two cases. The law of Moses consists of a collection of prescriptions which rule the social and religious life of an entire people, forming a set of civil procedures which tend to govern the entirety of life. Christ offered his followers "the law of the Spirit of life" (Rom 8:2), a law containing no rules for the civil and social sphere. Christ's law could not replace that of Moses, nor was such its intention. Jesus did not come "to destroy the law or the prophets but to bring them to their fulness" (Mt 5:17). What this means is that he came to infuse an interior spirit into the law and thus remove it from the intrinsic tendency to break down which is found in all legal formulations. Christ's new morality does not replace the Mosaic law (see Rom 3:31) but infuses it with meaning. It is not set out in external commands but rather is to be found written in the hearts of Christ's followers (see Rom 2:15).[23]

Christ's commands cannot be opposed to those of Moses or of the Jews as one law against another, but as the spirit against the law.[24] Such is the meaning of the counterpoint of the Sermon on the Mount: "You have heard that, . . . but I say to you. . . ." The three chapters of St. Matthew's Gospel devoted to this sermon can be seen as a kind of catechism for baptism for the early Christian community, with its leitmotif spelled out expressly in 5:20: "For I tell you, unless your righteousness exceeds that of the scribes and Pharisees, you will never enter the kingdom of heaven." The counterpoints thus appear as precepts of Christian morality going far beyond the Mosaic law, without any consequent assumption that this law has ceased to apply.[25]

[23] John L. McKenzie, in "The Law in the New Testament" in *The Jurist* (1966), p. 178, develops in depth the personalist and nonlegalistic meaning of the Christian norms: "There are some reasons for doubting that the principle of law has a meaningful function in the Christian life. One who would wish to define the 'common good' of the Church might find himself involved in impossible difficulties. The New Testament knows no other end of the Church than the incorporation of persons into Christ. The Church can have no accomplishment and no fulfilment which is not expressed in terms of individual persons."

[24] J. Jeremias (*Die Bergpredigt* [Stuttgart, Calwer, 1959], p. 15) notes that a legalistic interpretation of the Sermon on the Mount leads to contradictions incapable of being resolved.

[25] Such is the view of J. Jeremias in the book mentioned in the preceding note, a book which puts these observations in perspective.

When Jesus set out his standards for relations between brothers (Mt 5:21–26), he contrasted them with the Mosaic commandment, "You shall not kill," but this does not mean that he considered that this law has ceased to bind, or that he had any intention of substituting Christian courts for those of the civil authorities. The same comment can be made in broad terms of all the other contrasts presented in the Sermon on the Mount. One of these refers to the method of repudiation set out in Deuteronomy. The words used by Jesus to describe it were: "Whoever divorces his wife, let him give her a certificate of divorce" (Mt 5:31). What this Mosaic law actually did was to regulate the use of the right to divorce by setting up procedures favoring the wife and enabling her to pass under the protection of another husband. It was a far more humane law than those then current among other Semitic peoples.[26] But the new Christian morality made the legal instrument of the certificate of divorce practically useless by forbidding the Christian to use the right of repudiation except against a wife who had committed adultery. The Jewish provision was not abrogated, because it concerned a rule of social and civil life, and also because it served to protect the weaker party. But the one asking for baptism was notified of the moral rules governing the Christian community on this matter, rules surpassing in justice those of the scribes and the Pharisees.

The passages in Mark (10:1–12) and Matthew (19:3–12) which describe the conversation of Jesus and the Pharisees about divorce follow the same structure as the Sermon on the Mount but include a fuller development. To the law of Moses is opposed a new Christian concept which rises above it. This new concept is not directed to the Pharisees or to the general public but only to the disciples. This means that we are dealing with criteria which are valid for the internal life of the religious community in relation to the values flowing from the divine institution of marriage. But the legal provisions concerning the certificate of divorce remain untouched, because the Christian is allowed to avail himself of them in one specific situation, namely, adultery.

[26] Jeremias, *op. cit.*, p. 25.

The rules of the Christian community as set out in St. Paul and in the Gospels have and claim no force as regards the legal aspects of marriage.[27] Neither Jesus nor Paul takes a position concerning the validity or invalidity of repudiation and remarriage. The Christian rules do not bear on the marriage but on the moral worthiness and the community status of the one who violates them. The one who repudiates his wife without reason and remarries is judged an adulterer and as such expelled from the life of the community.[28] To use modern terms, the marriage was gravely illicit but not invalid. Besides, the notion of validity meant very little in the legal systems of early times, including the Roman.[29] The term *adulterer* as applied to the one who broke the Christian rule consequently lacks legal meaning, and that is why it was possible for Mark to apply it to the husband in relation to his wife (Mk 10:11).[30]

New Testament teaching offers a new concept of marriage which leaves no place for divorce or repudiation. Jesus refers to the same divine institution of a union of two in a single flesh or person, deducing therefrom an absolute moral rule: "What therefore God has joined together, let no man put asunder" (Mt 19:6). But the fact remains that man does separate them. Divorce has occurred everywhere and at all times. Jesus recognized this and offered an explanation. "Your hardness of heart" or infi-

---

[27] Some authors try to give a juridic character to the statement of Jesus by directing attention to the conditional form in which it is drafted, a form proper to the so-called "casuistic" laws (misphatim) of the Bible and of Eastern legal codes. See Dupont, *op. cit.*, p. 53.

[28] Later penitential discipline determined the length of this expulsion.

[29] According to Yaron, the different rabbinical schools in their disputes on divorce differed only as regards the moral judgment to be passed, not as regards the validity of the repudiation. In this view, the entire discussion between Jesus and the Pharisees would have been conducted on the moral level, without entering into the legal situation. See Yaron, "The Jewish Law of Divorce at the time of the New Testament," in *Marriage Breakdown, Divorce, Remarriage* (Toronto, 1962), p. 57. (Quoted by Pospishil, in *Divorce and Remarriage* (New York: Herder and Herder, 1967), p. 32.

[30] According to V. Taylor, *The Gospel according to St. Mark* (New York: St. Martins, 1952), p. 419, Mark's expression "refers to the first wife, and therefore goes beyond Jewish Law, in which a man can commit adultery against another married man but not against his own wife."

delity,[31] he said, was the reason why men repudiated their wives, thus calling for legislation to control and minimize as far as possible the effects of such hardheartedness. Jesus passes no judgment on this legislation, which is adapted to man's weakness, a weakness not eliminated by decree. What he does is to recall the integrity of the divine institution and propose it as the rule for his little flock, which—like the leaven in the dough—is to work on the world until it transforms it.

If Christ's teaching starts from a concept of marriage as indissoluble, it does not follow that he calls for a juridic and civil code of laws excluding divorce. The law of indissolubility is written on the heart of every Christian.[32] But society will always include nonbelievers as well as believers, and the Christian community itself will soon include "weak" as well as "strong" members.[33]

Throughout its pilgrimage on earth, the Church has to tolerate the weak who shelter in her bosom, together with their weaknesses and the consequences thereof. The hardness of heart which justified the Mosaic provision concerning repudiation will continue to affect many men, so that they will take advantage of it and of other provisions for divorce that may replace it.

That the teaching of Jesus rejecting divorce constitutes a moral ideal rather than a universally applicable rule is confirmed by the fact that an exception is immediately expressed. If Jesus had said simply that marriage could never be dissolved, nobody would try to find an exception. But Jesus restricts himself to urging (or commanding his followers) that man should not separate what God has joined. Indissolubility is not proclaimed like

---

31 The phrase Jesus used is "hardness of heart." R. A. Knox, *A New Testament Commentary for English Readers* (London, Sheed & Ward, 1953), Vol. I, p. 42, explains its meaning as follows: "Hardness of heart, in the language of the Scripture, is commonly used of rebelliousness, especially of the Jewish people against their God."

32 Gospel and law, in this sense, stand out antithetically against each other. As Harvey Cox says in *The Secular City*, "When Law rather than Gospel becomes the basis for our lives, it militates against choice and freedom. It decides for us, thus sapping our powers of responsibility. Similarly, Gospel in a broader sense means a summons to choice and answerability." (Macmillan, New York, 1965), p. 47.

33 Compare 1 Cor 8:11.

a physical law. It is offered as an ideal for all and a standard for the faithful. That is why Matthew could list an exception without altering the position of Jesus in any way.[34] The simple fact of introducing the exception brings the text of Matthew down to a legalist and casuistic plane far removed from that on which Jesus had spoken. It was an issue that might easily arise in the community. Was a faithful husband who repudiated an adulterous wife and remarried to be regarded as violating the standard proclaimed by Jesus? The negative answer to that question and its implications have already been analysed. It is here repeated simply to stress once more the difference between the rule proposed by Jesus and a juridic and legal ordinance.

Reference to an "ideal" proposed by Jesus is not to suggest that the members of his community were free to accept or reject his teaching on marriage. But the very way he expressed himself seems to limit his words to proposing an ideal. Thus, the statement that "from the beginning it was not so" (Mt 19:8) brings us back to the primeval paradise, the original state in which the ancients envisaged the first men to have lived. It was thought of as essentially different from the present state, with everything that related to that "beginning" as perfect by definition. Now Christ had come to reintroduce this perfection into the world, and in consequence he proposed it as an ideal for all men, but not as a law. Only within the community of the believers would the norms of Christ be fully observed, though without any compulsion. But what was true "in the beginning" would not be repeated in its entire perfection until "the end." The standard proposed by Christ is thus more than a counsel but less than a law. It is not a law, because the Christian community knows no laws of its own, limiting itself to observing human

---

[34] Most Catholic critics hold that the clause introducing the exception is an editorial addition of Matthew. Dupont does not think that conclusive proof of this view exists but he regards it as an acceptable position. See his comments on p. 92 of *Mariage et divorce dans l'Évangile*, as well as the substantial bibliography in that book. To attribute the formula of exception to Matthew himself would explain its casuistical and legalistic character, without lessening its authority. Crespy describes it as "an unfelicitous gloss" (*Le mariage*, p. 39). It would seem to indicate that in the very first Christian communities a legalistic view of the teachings of Jesus quickly developed.

laws with a renewed spirit. It is not a simple counsel, because it imposes an obligation in conscience and determines the situation of the believer with regard to the community.[35]

The words of Christ establish three distinct situations, all to be seen in "the present time." They are the Mosaic law,[36] the Christian norm, and the counsel. The permanence of a social law regulating divorce assumes a condition of sin which is a characteristic of the present "eon" or period. But faith in Christ conquers sin, and consequently there is installed inside the first situation a second one which excludes sin and consequently divorce, a situation strictly dependent on faith. In the third place, the counsel of perfect chastity creates a third enclosure in which is already to be found the first fruits of the escatological perfection, which is to say, the final goal of the Church. The three situations coexist, and each of them fulfills some of the needs of "the present time."

In this context, the concession to a husband to repudiate his

[35] This triple distinction between law, norm for the community and ideal seeks to escape the dilemma which soon faces all critics who start from the simple duality of law and ideal. To note the extreme positions, Brouwer believes that the statement of Jesus merely proposes an ideal (*De Bergrede* [Zeist, 1930], pp. 281ff), while Dupont (*op. cit.*, p. 54) insists that we are dealing with a legal decision. Bultmann and Taylor are close to Brouwer in insisting unduly on the individual aspect of the prescription laid down by Jesus (see the quotations in Dupont, p. 54, note 1). The view presented in the present book was inspired by the very reasonable observations of Georges Crespy (*op. cit.*, pp. 15–42), who makes the following comments regarding divorce: "Legitimate, permitted: these adjectives are applied to legal situations. But marriage is not a law, let us repeat, if we are to understand the words of Jesus aright" (p. 41). Our category of "a rule for the community" would have four characteristics. 1. It would fix the conditions for joining and remaining a member of the community. 2. It would obligate the believer in conscience. 3. It would not seek under any circumstances to be turned into a juridic prescription for the entire social group. 4. If it is desired to give it a juridic value within the community, it must not be forgotten that its binding force is linked essentially with the faith.

[36] The new alliance causes the old one to lapse, thus affecting its religious value but not changing the value of the prescriptions of Jewish law in so far as they regulate social life from the juridic viewpoint. This function, as far as the Christian community is concerned, is the same as that of human social laws. In consequence, the Mosaic law regarding the certificate of divorce had the same meaning for Jesus as do modern civil divorce codes for the Church.

wife because of her adultery and to remarry represents a regression to a lower situation, except that he is declared not to be responsible. The break, in fact comes as a result of sin and is understandable only in a sinful situation. The new marriage creates a kind of relationship for which there is no place in the new Christian morality, because it does not fit into any of its categories. Marriage, as a natural reality, acquires religious value if it measures up to the divine prototype proposed in paradise. But this new marriage following divorce does not measure up to that prototype and its religious Christian dimension will consequently have a different character. The community judges it to be lawful in certain cases, but it is not its primary type. Rather, it is a true exception to the rule, and later tradition will insist on pointing out that this is a concession to the "weakness" of man, including the believer, just as the authorization to the one whose spouse has died to remarry is also a concession. Of course, these considerations were tied to a determined anthropological state of affairs which no longer exists.

VI. Conclusions

1. The questions of exegesis raised by those texts of the gospels and of St. Paul which treat of divorce have not been resolved. In consequence, one cannot establish on the basis of Scripture either a theory that rejects divorce absolutely nor one that simply accepts it.

2. To formulate the question from the viewpoint of the validity or invalidity of the marriage or of the divorce is inadequate and anachronistic. The concepts implied in the scriptural passages in dispute are those of perfection-imperfection and lawfulness-unlawfulness.

3. In the New Testament, the marriage which measures up to the prototype instituted by God in paradise is the only one accorded the fulness of religious meaning, that is to say, a marriage which is absolutely one. To the extent that separation and remarriage withdraw from this prototype, they are also separated from the fulness of religious values in Christianity. In consequence, divorce and remarriage are unlawful for members of the Christian community, except in certain cases.

4. Neither Jesus nor Paul wanted the rules given for the Christian community to become legal valid precepts for the whole of society. The provision authorizing divorce and remarriage is appropriate to the actual stage of human development, so that everyone—including the Christian in certain exceptional cases—is entitled to avail himself of it.

CHAPTER 4

The First Ten Centuries

The history of the Church's attitude toward a breach of the marriage bond falls into two clearly distinguishable periods. The first stretches to the Peace of Constantine early in the fourth century. During that period the church did not feel the need to exercise an influence on civil and public life, limiting its entire activity to the Christian community. The standards proposed when dealing with questions of marriage and divorce were, in consequence, strictly religious and evangelical. The rules contemplated exclusively a community of believers brought together by voluntary acceptance of the faith and of a set of moral principles. They are strict rules, because they assume in the disciple of Christ a desire of perfection.

During this first phase, however, no theological reflection took place on marriage and its saving power. The rules laid down were based simply on the scripture texts taken literally and on a series of extremely rigorous moral and ascetic concepts. One seeks in vain in the patristic writings of the first three centuries for any proof that marriage was placed in a special religious, i.e., sacramental, category. Discussions of the theme were kept on the moral plane, naturally on the plane of Christian morality with its particular demands.

In the second phase, from the time of Constantine onwards, the Church began to think in social and legal terms. There are no longer simply Christian communities, but a Christian society to which everyone is gradually forced to belong. The Church then tried to adapt the evangelical norms to fit the needs of a public juridic order. The words of Jesus and of Paul were understood as legal pronouncements and, in consequence, given contradictory interpretations. The East understood the exceptive clause of the texts of St. Matthew as giving authority for a legal statute of limited divorce. The West held that it merely authorized a bodily separation of the spouses and introduced a law forbidding divorce for any reason. In both cases the projection of the words of scripture into an area for which they were not intended created an abusive situation by imposing an evangelical rule as a universal legal obligation on the whole of society.

Simultaneously, a timid but positive religious view of marriage began to develop in both the East and the West. This new dimension, by influencing the different legal provisions in the two areas, created situations of doctrinal incoherence which continued through the centuries. In the East, the sacramental character of marriage had to be acknowledged to unions which fulfilled the conditions prescribed by Church law, even when the theologians insisted that they did not express the religious values described by Jesus in the gospel. In the West, sacramentality and validity were fused into a single concept that dismissed every non-sacramental union as immoral.

For such reasons, a study of the patristic texts does not shed much doctrinal light. Their value as a guide in either the moral or the ecclesiastical sphere is limited by a moral and juridic context which differs radically from what contemporary Christian thought holds or assumes. Study of the Fathers should be almost exclusively historical and expository. Unless attempts at interpretation are very cautious, one is likely to build on tradition a dogmatic edifice totally lacking a worthwhile foundation.

The pages which follow contain the fruit of an effort of selecting and organizing a mass of historical documents. To facilitate reading, I have placed in the notes all observations and quotations which might break the thread of the discussion. Nevertheless, the importance of the issues make it impossible to rush quickly through the historical evidence concerning divorce.

The historical study deals not only with the remarriage of the innocent abandoned spouse but with the issue of divorce in general. The patristic references, especially in the first centuries, tend to be imprecise and general. An overall view is possible only by broadening the field of study. Accordingly, all situations in which the marriage bond seems to be dissolved will be included. It is proper to note, nevertheless, that the case of the innocent abandoned spouse seems to occupy a place of privilege in the complex world of prohibitions, permissions, and counsels which the study seeks to penetrate.

I. General Rules of Historical Interpretation

The first point to note is the presence of a rule and an exception. An objective study of the Christian documents of the first ten centuries produces two definite facts. On the one side, there is unanimity in proclaiming that Christian marriage cannot be dissolved. On the other, there is the fact that many of these same testimonies explicitly recognize an exception on the ground of adultery by one spouse.

Catholic theologians since Trent refuse to accept such a gross contradiction on the part of the Fathers of the Church, and they accordingly deny that they admitted such an exception. This they do by forcing an "orthodox" meaning on the old texts favoring remarriage so that they cease to contradict the current practice of the Church of Rome.[1] The Fathers of Trent were here more liberal when they explicitly admitted that some of the early Church Fathers had recognized an exception to the rule of indissolubility.[2]

---

[1] Most authors of manuals of theology follow Perrone, *De Matrimonio Christiano* (Rome, 1858), Vol. 3, pp. 240ff. Huarte's conclusion is that "the Greeks cannot claim the teaching of the Fathers of the Church in favor of their view, but only the civil legislation" (*Tractatus de Ordine et Matrimonio* [Rome, 3rd edition, 1931] p. 192).

[2] Pedro Guerrero, Archbishop of Granada, cites as authorities favoring divorce the councils of Elvira, Arles and Toledo, the Apostolic Canons, Theodoretus, Ambrose, Lactantius, Theophilactus, Epiphanius, Cromatius, John Chrysostom, Hilary, Tertullian, Basil, Burchard of Worms, and Pope Gregory II. His conclusion: "Non placet igitur quod sancti doctores damnentur," meaning that he was opposed to the proposed canon because it would condemn these Church Fathers. See S. Ehses, *Concilii Tridentini Actorum pars sexta* (Freiburg, 1924), p. 689. Modern theologians of Eastern Churches in union with Rome also agree that some patristic authorities favor divorce. Patriarch Maximos IV Saigh, for example, told *La Croix*, October 3, 1965, that "the contrary practice of the Eastern Churches can find support in some statements of some Church Fathers."

A scientifically exact historical interpretation should provide an explanation that will not involve altering established facts. Interpretations of the teaching of the early Church on marriage should respect the conclusions of objective historical study. In the present instance, the statements on indissolubility and those on the existence of an exception should be accorded a single and coherent explanation. Such an explanation exists. In order to neutralize the often unconscious tendency of the Catholic reader to apply modern theological categories to documents written in another period and in a different perspective, it is appropriate to outline this explanation before proceeding to an analysis of the patristic texts.

When an early Christian writer speaks of marriage, the first point to determine is the audience for which what he says is intended. The Christian masters did not present their teaching in the same way to the faithful and to pagans. On the contrary, a striking difference exists between a catechetical treastise directed to the faithful and a kerygmatic document intended for missionary preaching. When Christian teachers addressed pagans, the most important thing was to stress the contrast between the corruption and laxity of marriage practices in the Greek and Roman world and the uprightness of Christian marriage. Within this framework, the affirmations simultaneously provide contrasts.

Two lay writers of the second century compared in detail the high morality of Christian practices and pagan corruption. Justin, the Christian who wrote as a philosopher, argues in favor of Christian uprightness by listing the teachings of Christ on chastity. He then adds: "It follows that, for our Master, not only those are sinners who enter a double marriage in conformity with human law, but also those who look at a woman to covet her." A little later, he contrasts the continence of young Christians with the dissolute life exemplified by Antinoüs, the favorite of the emperor Hadrian.[3]

Athenagoras, the Athenian philosopher, addresses an appeal to the emperors and denounces the widespread contemporary de-

---

[3] Justinus, I *Apologia*, 15 and 29.

pravity in an effort to stress the balance and honesty of the creed of the Christians. In the heat of the argument, he presents as the Christian law what is merely its special ascetic strictness: "The man who separates from his first wife, even when she has died, is a secret adulterer." Athenagoras fails to mention that Paul authorized the remarriage of one whose spouse had died, trying in this way to impress his pagan readers with an image of Christianity with extremely rigorous laws governing sex relationships.[4]

It is easy to collect other patristic texts affirming indissolubility pure and simple. The Christians were completely convinced that the moral level of their teachings was the best argument in favor of their superiority. Its high respect for chastity was thus the most obvious ornament of the new religion, so that it became the practice to stress the most novel and rigorous aspects, namely, perfect continence and indissolubility of marriage.

It would be mistaken, nevertheless, to jump from this abundance of evidence to the conclusion that the Fathers excluded absolutely the possibility of divorce and remarriage. The scope of the affirmation of indissolubility must be determined by the general context of the period. The Fathers contrasted Christian and pagan practices, this at a time when both Roman law and Jewish custom permitted divorce for various reasons, even by simple agreement of the parties. Repudiation and remarriage were frequent in the society ruled by the imperial laws, and the extreme ease of divorce tended to corrupt the institution of marriage. A teaching which eliminated divorce by consent and permitted separation only within narrow limits appeared consequently as the champion of indissolubility of marriage, or at least as a challenge to Roman divorce legislation. To permit a number of exceptions to the general principle did not invalidate the strong position taken by the Christian law and did not weaken its overall thrust. A Christian could boldly declare that marriage was indissoluble while admitting, for example, the exception provided in the case of a wife's adultery.

What is more, the exception for adultery could not be denied

[4] Athenagoras, *Legatio*, 33.

by Christians without introducing a teaching harmful to the institution of marriage. Adultery by a wife was severely punished by Roman law. The new religion could not introduce a principle that allowed the guilty one to go free, and to forbid the innocent party to remarry would be to favor the adulterous one. This was so obvious that most Christian writers took it for granted or mentioned it only in passing.

Actually, nevertheless, most of the old texts cited in favor of indissolubility mention the exception in the case of adultery. This is true even of such rigorous authors as Tertullian, who wrote that "Christ allowed repudiation for one reason only, namely, when what it was sought to avoid—adultery—had already occurred."[5] Clement of Alexandria claims that the exception in Matthew (19:9) does not alter the universality of Christ's prescription: "Scripture establishes a law that one who takes a wife can never leave the marriage: you shall not expel your wife, except for adultery."[6] The same ambivalence is found in Lactantius, a Latin writer of the fourth century. He proclaims the divine institution of an indissoluble marriage bond, while admitting dissolution for adultery. "However, as the wife is constrained by the obligation of chastity not to desire another man, so also the man is held to the same law, because God has joined man and wife in the bond of only one body. He commanded therefore not to dismiss a wife unless she is proven guilty of adultery, and that the bond of the conjugal contract should never be dissolved except that which perfidy has broken."[7]

Such statements by the Church Fathers should not, however, be taken as automatically proving that the innocent abandoned spouse is free to remarry. But they at least show that the Fathers did not forbid remarriage. They make it clear that simply to collect patristic texts affirming the indissolubility of marriage will not exclude the possibility of exceptions to that rule. That was the mistake made by post-Tridentine theologians. They gave the statements of the early Fathers a scope they did not possess, turning their teaching on the permanence of the marriage

5 *De Monogamia*, 9. In Migne's *Patrologia Latina* (hereafter PL) 2, 991.
6 *Stromata*, II, 23, 145, 3.
7 *Divine Institutiones*, 46, PL 6, 1080.

bond into an absolute rule permitting no exception. They then drew two conclusions, both quite gratuitous. First, they said that when the Fathers spoke of divorce, they referred merely to "the physical or bodily separation"[8] of the spouses. Second, they said that examples of toleration of remarriage resulted only from occasional relaxations of discipline.

A study of the historical tradition free from any assumptions must take into account only those testimonies which either allow or reject remarriage of Christians clearly. In the light of what has been already said, a simple statement that marriage is indissoluble is not to the point.

1. *Various cases and circumstances*

To speak of divorce and remarriage is to oversimplify. The history of Christianity provides no elaboration of doctrinal teaching on this subject until the late Middle Ages, other than some tentative proposals of St. Augustine. The Fathers and the early councils all dealt with specific cases and never offered a general survey of the situation. It is consequently all important to identify and define the many possible ways in which the bond can be broken and remarriage occur, before analyzing the historic testimonies. It is surprising how few of those who discuss the subject take this elementary step.

The number of different possible cases can easily be determined by a simple mathematical operation, combining each of the spouses with all the possible circumstances. The possibilities are as follows:

1. Remarriage of husband and of wife.
2. Each spouse can be either innocent or guilty:
   a. innocent husband;
   b. guilty husband;
   c. innocent wife;
   d. guilty wife.
3. The ground for divorce can be either adultery or something else:

---

[8] The obvious meaning of divorce is the total dissolution of the marriage permitting a new marriage. In *Etimologiae*, L. IX, 7, 25, St. Isidore of Seville says: "Divorce occurs when, after a marriage has been dissolved, one of the parties contracts a new marriage."

    a. innocent husband, separation on ground of adultery;

    b. innocent husband, separation for reason other than adultery;

    c. guilty husband, separation on ground of adultery;

    d. guilty husband, separation for reason other than adultery;

    e. innocent wife, separation on ground of adultery;

    f. innocent wife, separation for reason other than adultery;

    g. guilty wife, separation on ground of adultery;

    h. guilty, separation for reason other than adultery.

At least eight possibilities, accordingly, must be taken into account when evaluating each text taken from tradition. Any study of the evolution of Catholic teaching which fails to take these distinctions into account can be called arbitrary and superficial, and its conclusions will lack weight. The legitimacy of these criteria for distinguishing the various situations will appear as the issues are developed.

2. *Roman civil legislation on divorce*

Under the Roman empire, marriage as a juridic entity was a contract which could at any time be cancelled by the parties (*divortium ex consensu*). The laws of Augustus[9] in the first century and the decrees of Constantine[10] in the fourth limited the right of repudiation (*ius repudii*) without significantly changing the rules for divorce by mutual consent. That situation continued substantially until the sixth century, when Theodosius the Younger and Justinian considerably restricted divorce by consent to the point of almost eliminating this ground.[11] They also formulated the grounds for repudiation, seven against the wife and five against the husband.[12] In all cases, those divorced were allowed to remarry.

---

[9] *Lex Julia de adulteriis coercendis,* and *Lex Papia Poppaea.* See "Divorce" in *Encyclopedia Britannica.*

[10] Causes for repudiating a husband listed in the Constantinian code were homicide, poisoning and violation of graves. Those for repudiating a wife were adultery, poisoning and procuring. See *Decreta Constantiniana,* "De Repudiis," PL 8, 353-354.

[11] Granted only for impotency on the part of the man, entrance into religion, and captivity. Later, the two who separated had to enter monasteries.

[12] See *Nomocanon,* tit. 13, chapter 4 (Pitra, II, 614). The causes are listed in "Divorce" in *Encyclopedia Britannica.*

Adultery, understood as an extramarital relation of a married woman with a man, was forbidden and severely punished by imperial legislation. The adulteress was executed or exiled, as was her accomplice. This concept of adultery, with its legal consequences, was not applied to the husband. An extramarital relationship of a husband with an unmarried woman was considered as fornication only and was not a crime. The basic juridic inequality of the sexes, which existed also—as noted above—in Jewish law, is a factor of the highest importance for a right understanding of the Christian documents written at a time while Roman law was still in force. This legal status will be discussed later.

Our previous contention that a teaching which completely excluded divorce by consent and kept the grounds for repudiation to a minimum could rightly claim to defend the indissolubility of the marriage bond becomes more intelligible in this light.

3. *The Christian doctrinal context*

The Christian moral demands and the way they were presented to the pagans have already been described. It is now appropriate to see the immediate doctrinal context of the Christian discipline regarding marriage, in order to understand better the expressions used by the writers, and in order to avoid hasty or mistaken interpretations.

Christian sexual morality in the first centuries was dominated by the idea of *encrateia* or continence. Carried to its extreme, this notion gave rise to heretical encratism and rejected all marriage as a corruption unworthy of the Christian. The Church Fathers always defended the lawfulness of marriage in the Christian economy, but their moral teaching is tainted to a greater or lesser degree by encratism. One finds a very broad spectrum of attitudes in Christian writers, ranging from the modern-sounding equilibrium of Clement of Alexandria to the extreme rigorism of Origen, Methodius, and Augustine.

A strange example of the variety of opinions is found in an exchange of correspondence preserved by the historian Eusebius. He tells that Bishop Dionysius of Corinth (first century) wrote a letter to the faithful of Cnosos "in which he urged the bishop of that Church, Pinitos, not to impose as an obligation on the brethren the heavy burden of continence, taking account of the weakness of the majority. Pinitos replied with expressions of his admiration for Dionysius and his approval of the advice Dionysius had given him. He was, he said, encouraged to give more solid food by means of better writings to the undernourished people under his care.[13] This all means that Pinitos had been imposing continence on his followers without being judged a heretic. Within Christian orthodoxy there was room for the rigors of a moral asceticism which gave little account to the values of married life.

Popular Christianity remained for many centuries under the influence of such encratic ideas. The apocryphal books of the New Testament are in considerable part encratic.[14] The famous *Passion of St. Tecla*, a kind of Christian novel of the second century, presents Paul's teaching in Iconium as strictly encratic. "There will be no resurrection for you unless you remain chaste and avoid defiling your bodies."[15] The author of this work was a priest from Asia Minor who was expelled from his post for having assumed it illegally, but not for heresy.[16]

A more or less orthodox encratism could plead the support of St. Paul (1 Cor 7) and still more the shocking expression of Revelation: "It is these who have not defiled themeselves with women" (14:4). Most Christian pastors, nevertheless, presented a consistent equilibrium by describing marriage as good and continence as better.[17] When the Gnostics and Manicheans elevated encratism to the status of a system, Catholics were more careful to reject it. Traces survived, nevertheless, throughout the entire historic period right down to the present time.

The moral demands of early Christianity were tied into a broader doctrinal context by the distinction between "the per-

---

[13] Eusebius, *Historia Ecclesiastica*, IV, 23, 7.
[14] For example, *Actus Petri cum Simone, Acta Andreae, Acta Thomae*. See Johannes Quasten, *Patrology* (Westminster, Md.: The Newman Press, 1953), I, 135–139.
[15] No. 12 of the old Latin version published by Oscar von Gebhardt, *Texte und Untersuchungen*, 22, 2.
[16] Tertullian, *De Baptismo*, 17. PL 1, 1329.
[17] For example, *II Clem.*, 15; Polycarp. *ad Phil.*, II, 4–5.

fect" and "the imperfect." Christian historians have always shown themselves suspicious of this distinction, claiming that it had arisen from a Gnostic deviation. It is clear, however, that this ascetico-moral teaching is also found in an orthodox version in nearly all early Christian writers.

In the third century, Christian Gnosticism succeeded in establishing a special category of the faithful, the perfect or spiritual, as contrasted with the imperfect or the carnal. This distinction toned down the exaggerations of Gnosticism and Montanism, but it led to its own kind of arbitrariness. Clement of Alexandria held that the passage from simple faith to *gnosis* or spiritual knowledge was a conversion, and that the Gnostics would have a separate place in heaven.[18] Origen said that those of simple faith know the Word made flesh whereas the Gnostics know the eternal Word.[19] Methodius of Olympus (3rd century) provides a typical text: "Here it is also clear that he wishes to teach us that the virgins were restricted to this number, that is, to 144,000, whereas the multitude of the rest of the saints is beyond counting. Note what he teaches us as he considers the others: I also saw a great multitude which no man could number, of every tongue and tribe and of every nation. Obviously, then, as I have said, he introduces an untold number in the case of the other saints, but only a very small number in the case of the virgins, as though he deliberately intended a contrast with the larger, uncounted number."[20] The Christian Gnostic did not deny that the married could be saved, but he excluded them from the path leading to the pinnacle of perfection.

Continence was an essential component of Christian perfection. It was contrasted with the "weakness"[21] which drove man to marriage and which justified the married state. Such teaching left room for little sympathy for married life and its values. St. Paul had already written that "it is better to marry than to be aflame with passion" (1 Cor 7:9). What married people got

---

[18] *Stromata*, VI, 15, 131–132, and VI, 14, 108–114.
[19] *In Jo. Comm.*, II, 3, 27–31.
[20] *Symposium*, I, 5. In Ancient Christian Writers (herefater A.C.W.) 27, 48.
[21] "Let the strong not ignore the weak." (*I Clem.*, 38, 2).

most were frequent urgings to limit the use of marriage: "In the same way as the farmer, when he has placed the seed in the ground, waits for the harvest and does not continue to plant, so for you the measure of your desire is the procreation of children."[22] The sex act was regarded with much suspicion. According to Tertullian, "it is unthinkable that in heaven God would offer his friends a thing so frivolous and dirty as conjugal pleasure."[23] St. Augustine, for his part, voices an opinion which will be repeated throughout the Middle Ages: "It is one thing to have sex relations for the exclusive purpose of producing offspring, in which case there is no fault. It is something else to seek voluptuous pleasure in union with one's spouse, and that is a venial sin."[24] Subsequently, local councils forbade spouses who recently had carnal relations to receive Communion.

When these facts are taken into account, it is no surprise to learn that the rules governing the institution of marriage were strict and demanding during the whole of the early period of Christianity. For that reason, concessions and permissions become all the more noteworthy because of the hostile climate with which they have to contend. Remarriage of one whose spouse has died provides a good example.

St. Paul allowed but did not recommend remarriage after the death of a spouse. He even excluded those married several times from the office of bishop.[25] The Western Fathers followed his lead rather closely. Tertullian showed a dislike for remarriage in his writings while he was a Catholic, and he forbade it completely during his Montanist period.[26] The Greek Fathers are ambiguous. One gets the impression that only the explicit toleration of Paul prevented them from roundly condemning remarriage. They compensated by imposing heavy penances on those who remarried.[27]

---

[22] Athenagoras, *Legatio*, 33.
[23] *Ad Uxorem* (written while still a Catholic), I, 1. PL 1, 1389.
[24] *De Nuptiis et Concupiscentia*, I, 15. PL 44, 423.
[25] 1 Cor 7:39; 1 Tim 3:2; Tit 1:5–7
[26] *Ad Uxorem* (Catholic period); *De Monogamia* (Montanist period).
[27] For example, one or two years for a second marriage, three or four for a third (Basilius, *Epist. can.*, 188, 4. In Migne's *Patrologia Graeca* (hereafter PG) 32, 292).

Another very interesting aspect of the question of remarriage after death of a spouse is that various Fathers discuss it at the same time as that of remarriage after divorce. When this is understood, it is possible to interpret in favor of the possibility of divorce some texts concerning bigamy which are doubtful or excessively general. The extreme position of Athenagoras, for whom both situations deserve to be called "decent adultery," has already been mentioned. Tertullian criticizes some women who remarry "after divorce or the death of their husband," and he recalls that Leviticus legislated at the same time for the widow and the repudiated wife.[28] The phrase of Clement of Alexandria is decisive: "The woman guilty of fornication lives for sin but is dead to the commandments."[29] But the most interesting text is that of Asterius of Amasea (4th century), who goes so far as to say that he understands remarriage better in the case of abandonment than in that of death, adding: "Marriage is dissolved only by death and by adultery."[30] The conclusion to be drawn is that every mention of tolerance for remarriage in general is to be understood as including remarriage after divorce. That means a substantial increase in the number of pertinent texts.

The history of the teaching concerning remarriage thus appears as yet another episode in the continuing tension between what the Fathers considered as the Christian ideal and the "tolerations" introduced by Scripture and the traditions of the Churches.

To sum up, these points must be kept in mind in attempting an interpretation of the teaching of the Fathers on divorce and remarriage:

1. To affirm that marriage is indissoluble does not exclude the possibility of exceptions to the rule.

2. In regard to each patristic statement, it is necessary to specify as clearly as possible the circumstances of the situation to which it refers (husband, wife, innocent, guilty, etc.).

---

[28] *Ad Uxorem*, II, 1. PL 1, 1401. *De Monogamia*, 7. PL 2, 938.

[29] *Stromata*, II, 23, 147. Clement is dealing here with the text of Matthew (5:32) which he quotes in full, including the clause making an exception for adultery.

[30] *Homilia in Matthaeum*, 19, 3. PG 40, 238.

3. The laws of the Roman empire established juridic equality for the husband and the wife.

4. A substratum of encratism is found to a greater or lesser extent in all the literature of early Christianity.

II. Before Constantine

In addition to being a sacramental or religious reality, marriage is a social institution governed by juridic regulations. Modern Catholicism presents its own juridic order for marriage, the fruit of a long process which began with the political and religious transformation affected by Constantine and which obliged the Church to express itself in the legal sphere. During the second and third centuries, by contrast, the Church had evolved under primarily religious and ideological pressures, with little concern for public life. Teaching on marriage during those early centuries was principally religious in character and it was motivated by strictly Christian considerations. In consequence, it represents for the present purposes a testimony of incalculable value.

As regards the discipline governing remarriage, the pre-Nicene Fathers exhibit a stable balance resulting from the action of two opposing forces. One was the encratic tendency urging moral rigorism, and the other was the evangelical and apostolic tradition in favor of moderation and tolerance. The varying pressures of the two forces produced some slight oscillation, but the equilibrium tended normally to be quite workable.

Among Christian writers of the second and third centuries, Hermas seems to be the only one to deny explicitly the right to remarry on grounds of adultery, but even this text must be taken with reserve.[31] Other writers referring to the indissolu-

31 *Pastor* belongs to the apocalyptic literary genus and seeks to explain the notion of Christian penance. Commandment 4 includes this rule; "Hermas said to the messenger of God: If one have a wife who believes in the Lord, and if he apprehends her in adultery, does he commit sin if he lives with her? And he said to me: He does not commit a sin as long as he is unaware of this misconduct, but if, knowing of the misconduct, the husband lives with his wife without her doing penance, he participates in her sin and her adultery. What, then, shall the husband do, O Lord, if his wife persists in this passion? And the Lord replied: Let him put her away and let the husband abide alone; but if, after putting

bility of marriage either mention or assume the exception on the basis of the wife's adultery. Some texts of Tertullian, Clement of Alexandria, and Origen deserve more detailed examination.

Trying to show that there are no fundamental conflicts between the law of Moses and that of Christ, Tertullian asserts in his book against Marcion that "the justification of divorce has even Christ as a defender." The difference introduced by Christ, says Tertullian, is that the one ground he accepts as valid is adultery on the part of the wife. The whole context shows that the discussion is about complete divorce as granted by the Mosaic law, that is to say, divorce permitting remarriage.[32] There is no need to comment further on this text. Such Catholic authors as Lercher, Esmein, Bartmann and Diekamp agree that it favors divorce. But Tertullian has less-known remarks which are even more significant because they belong to his Montanist period and are found in the work in which condemns absolutely the remarriage of one whose spouse has died. Christ, he wrote, "allowed repudiation for one cause and only one, namely, when what it is desired to avoid (adultery) has already occurred." "*We*, however," he added, "even if we repudiate, are not permitted to remarry."[33] "We" here indicates the Montanists, the "paracletes," in scathing opposition to the Catholics who are by inference recognized as allowing remarriage in such circumstances.

---

away his wife, he shall marry another, he likewise commits adultery. . . . For the sake of her repentance, therefore, the husband ought not to marry." Hermas seems here to be arguing against one of the consequences of not admitting a second penance after baptism, namely, that the offended husband could not hope for the return of his wife and would consequently remarry immediately. Hermas obliges him to wait for the guilty one, in case she should repent, as follows from his final remark.

[32] "I assert that Christ forbade divorce conditionally, that is to say, in the case in which a man dismisses his wife *in order to* marry another. . . . In consequence, the marriage which has not been properly (*rite*) dissolved remains; and if the marriage remains, it is adulterous to remarry. Thus, if he forbade a man to send his wife away under certain circumstances, he did not forbid this absolutely; and if he did not forbid it absolutely, that means that he allowed it in some circumstances, namely, when the reason for which he forbade it does not apply" (Tertullian, *Adversus Marcionem*, 4, 34. PL 2, 473ff).

[33] *De Monogamia*, 9. PL 2, 991.

An often misquoted passage from Clement of Alexandria's *Stromata* deserves to be restudied in its total context. It occurs in a chapter[34] devoted to a reply to the encratics and Gnostics who condemned marriage. Clement's opponents were relying on the text of Matthew (19:11–12) in which Jesus recommends virginity. Clement replied that this counsel of Jesus was not directed to all, because "some" (the disciples) has questioned him in private after his discussion with the Pharisees, wanting to know if a man could marry another woman when his first wife had been found guilty of adultery and divorced. And Jesus had answered with the statement which the Gnostics and encratics had completely misinterpreted: "Not all men can receive this precept, but only those to whom it is given" (Mt 19:11). What this means, according to Clement, is that the counsel of chastity proposed by Jesus is directed only to those who contemplate remarriage after a wife's adultery and not to marriage in general. Continence is urged on the innocent spouse not as a precept but as a counsel.

Origen, one of the most influential Christian writers of all times, discusses at length the text of Matthew (19:3–12) concerning divorce. One brief passage of Origen's commentary, a passage which is absolutely meaningless if taken out of its context, is the cause of endless conflict among Catholic theologians. Of the 25 books of the *Commentary on the Gospel of St. Matthew* written by Origen in Cesarea after the year 244, only 8 survive in the original Greek. One full chapter is devoted to an explanation of Matthew 19:1–12, and the reader is quickly struck by the acuteness of the perception and the lofty spiritual tone.[35] After a minute analysis of the gospel text, Origen offers a spiritual explanation of the "certificate of divorce." Christ, he says, has repudiated the synagogue and taken a new wife, the Church. In doing this, nevertheless, he has not broken his Father's command that no man should put asunder what God had joined together, because the synagogue had committed adul-

---

[34] *Stromata*, III, 6, 50. The entire context of this Chapter 6 is worth studying.
[35] Origen, *In Mattheum Commentarium*, 14, 16–24. PG, 13, 1224ff (GCS 38, 321ff).

tery by separating from him.[36] One could already conclude merely from these speculations of Origen that his readers took for granted that a man who repudiated his adulterous wife and remarried did not break the Lord's commandment.

Origen, however, makes the point even more explicitly. In the scriptures, he says, are to be found laws based not on a transcendental ideal but on the divine condescendence which takes the weakness of those subject to the law into account. This double dimension of law "is found also in the New Testament, in which certain laws are framed on the model of the one which says that for your hardness of heart Moses allowed you to divorce your wives. Precisely because of our[37] hardness of heart and thanks to our weakness, St. Paul wrote such rules as the one which says that—a wife is bound to her husband as long as he lives, but if the husband dies, she is free to be married to whom she wishes— (1 Cor 7:39)."

Immediately afterwards, Origen refers to a certain practice of the Church in his time which did not seem to agree literally with the Pauline prescriptions regarding the remarriage of the woman. "Even now, here acting outside of holy Scripture, some superiors of the Church have permitted a woman to marry while her husband is alive; they act most assuredly outside of holy Scripture in which we read, 'The wife is bound for her lifetime to her husband,' and 'The wife will be considered adulterous if she, during the lifetime of her husband, joins up with another man.' Yet they did not act without reason, because, so it seems, they have accorded condescension outside of what had been prescribed and transmitted in order to prevent worse consequences."[38] Such extreme tolerance, although not foreseen in the scripture, is judged by Origen not to lack a reasonable justifica-

---

[36] N. 17, PG 1231.

[37] Delarue, the author of the Latin translation of the Migne edition, translates: "*their* hardness of heart," thereby weakening the impact of the expression.

[38] N. 23, PG 1245. Delarue translates *symperiphora* (condescension) as "alieno arbitrio morem gerentes," that is to say, as "acting on the basis of the judgment of others." It is only a short step from this translation to the conclusion that Origen was criticizing the civil laws, a step taken by Perrone, followed by Huarte and Pesch.

98   *The Abandoned Spouse*

tion. What is most notable about the text is that the authorization given by the bishops in question, although it goes beyond the limits set by Paul to his tolerance, suffices for Origen to deny that the woman so favored is guilty of adultery. We have here a testimony to a practice of remarriage based on purely pastoral considerations, and its only basis in scripture is the general teaching regarding the divine condescendence for human weakness.

This passage from Origen cannot in any case be presented as evidence for the aboslute indissolubility of marriage. Even if the condemnatory expressions used by Origen concerning the lax bishops are forced to their limits, only the situation of the wife is at issue. The husband is not mentioned.

The difference of marriage discipline as regards the husband and the wife is implicitly accepted by Origen when he offers a literal interpretation of Mt 19:9: "Our Lord does not permit dissolution for any cause other than the established fornication of the wife." And the reason he gives for narrowing the grounds of divorce to adultery alone is as follows: "Every husband who repudiates his wife places her in the occasion of committing adultery, naturally excluding the case when she is already an adulteress." And this leads to Origen's overall conclusion: "A woman is an adulteress if she marries while her husband is still alive, and a man is an adulterer if he marries a woman who has been repudiated."[39]

To sum up Origen's teaching, remarriage is permitted by the divine condescension, but a wife may not remarry as long as her husbaand is alive. The simple fact of mentioning the limitation for the wife shows that this limitation does not exist for the husband. For him there is a different limitation. He can repudiate his wife and remarry only if she commits adultery.[40]

The Christian writers of the second and third centuries presented this as the common and unchanging belief of the Church. All without exception regarded the state of virginity as higher

[39] *In Matthaeum Commentarium*, 14, 24.
[40] It must be re-emphasised that, in the scriptural as well as in the legal context, "repudiation" meant perfect divorce with authorization of remarriage of the innocent party. The wife could also ask for a simple "bodily" separation and adultery was by no means the only ground for such a demand.

than marriage and tended to limit man's sex activity. They also recognized a general rule of condescension for the weakness of the flesh. But when it came to concrete issues of tolerance, they stuck close to the letter of the scriptures. They tolerated with St. Paul remarriage of one whose spouse had died, and with the Lord divorce on the ground of the wife's adultery. They allowed nothing more, not the slightest concession. On the contrary, these concessions were made at times with the greatest reluctance, and they quickly protested if pastoral applications showed the least sign of going farther. Modified encratism continued to exert a secret pressure, giving to the moral teaching of those centuries a coloring which placed it somewhere between that of the gospel and that of the Stoics.

On the other hand, there is no sign of any effort to stress the religious values attributed to marriage in the Bible. This era knows no theology of marriage which develops the teaching of Jesus and the teaching of St. Paul in his letter to the Ephesians. Indissolubility is justified on moral grounds, and the limits placed on the exceptions are not based on the mysterious concept of the union of the spouses but on the ascetic drive to curb the activity of the flesh.

III. THE EAST AFTER NICEA

The very special kind of equilibrium which prevailed in the period preceding the Council of Nicea was broken in two directions as a result of the Church's entry into public and official life. The simplicity of the old system collapsed under the weight of the new tensions. On the one hand, the gospel law as such was intended to rule the life of necessarily small religious communities for which a certain level of strictness was permissible. On the other hand, the new situation called on the Church to make rules for a large mass of members whose religious development was quite low, and later also to set the spirit of the laws of civil society. The East overcame the tension by bringing the ecclesiastical customs into line with the civil laws, thus establishing a new equilibrium at a level of lower moral demands. The West reacted in a diametrically opposite way. It struggled to transform the civil laws to fit the molds of the religious and moral teaching developed by its theologians and practiced by its monks.

The incorporation of the civil rules for marriage and divorce into the ecclesiastical customs of the East was gradual. Simultaneously, and in particular from the time of Justinian, the imperial legislation tried to draw closer to the Christian ideals, limiting the causes of divorce and all but eliminating divorce by consent.[41] The process did not take place, however, without conflict. The theologian bishops of the fourth and fifth centuries constantly criticized the laws of the Christian emperors of the East and urged the faithful not to model their lives on them. The ecclesiastical canons and the civil laws governing marriage coexisted for a long time, provoking unending disputes and interference of one power with the other. Only the authority of the code known as the *Novellae Justiniani* promulgated in the sixth century smothered the last protests, so that divorce was accepted once for all by the Eastern Church.

For two centuries the leaders of the Christian people had used all their efforts to maintain what has here been called "the pre-Nicene equilibrium," the teaching, namely, that marriage is one and indissoluble, apart from the exceptions specified in the scriptures. The explanations of the phrase in St. Matthew regarding the certificate of divorce are clearly based on what Origen had said. Basil, Epiphanius, Gregory Nazianzen, John Chrysostom and Asterius are equally assiduous in defending the purity of the Christian teaching.[42] But two new elements within the Christian community itself are steadily eroding their base. One is the growing laxity of ecclesiastical practice, and the other is the reflection taking place on the notion of natural law.

---

[41] See above, p. 88.

[42] Some exegetes were stricter. Theodore of Mopsuestia (5th century) comments as follows on Matthew's phrase regarding divorce: "In appearance, (the repudiated wife) remains separated from her husband, but in reality she is his body once for all, since by marriage God adapted and adjusted her to her husband, in such a way that they are now one single flesh. In consequence, neither can the husband marry another." See J. Reuss, *Matthäus—Kommentare aus der griechischen Kirche, aus Katenenhandschriften gesammelt und herausgegeben*, T.U., 61, Berlin, 1957. Fr. 3, on Mat 5:32. However, the context of this exegesis is missing, so that it is not possible to determine its thrust.

Witnesses to the purest teaching tradition are John Chrysostom and Asterius of Amasea. There is no point in dwelling at length on what they say about marriage and divorce, because they merely repeat with a renewed theological vigor the firm conviction of the previous centuries, namely, that the Lord limited the granting of divorce to the one ground of the wife's adultery. And here more than anywhere else it is proper to recall that the word *repudiation* always meant for these bishops separation with the right of remarriage for the innocent man. The fact is that what they say is part of a continuous dispute with the "external" (civil) laws which allowed remarriage for all cases of repudiation.[43]

The impact of their reflection on the natural bases of divorce is notable in Gregory Nazianzen and Epiphanius. This is how Gregory presents the Christian teaching on repudiation: "The Mosaic law grants a certificate of divorce for any cause. But Christ does not allow it for any cause. He limits it to the situation in which a husband separates from an immodest and adulterous wife."[44] What is interesting is that he goes on to protest the inequality of husband and wife before the law, a point which seemed to concern his predecessors very little. Recalling that the Jewish laws (like those of Rome) branded the infidelity of the wife but not that of the husband as adultery, he commented:

[43] Here are the most important texts. Asterius of Amasea (circa 400) says of those who change a wife as easily as a suit of clothes: "This you should hold as established and be entirely persuaded of, that marriage can be dissolved for no cause whatever, except because of death and adultery" (*Homilia in Matthaeum*, 19, 3. PG 40, 225). Asterius goes on to say that he excuses more easily the remarriage of the innocent husband than that of one whose spouse has died (*Ibid.*, PG 237). John Chrysostom recalls repeatedly the prohibition against the wife's remarriage during her husband's lifetime. But he never says the same law applies to the husband. On the contrary, he says quite clearly that he can lawfully remarry in case of adultery: "You could rest quite tranquil if you saw that St. Paul allowed you to expel from your home a wife loaded with defects, and remarry. But he does not allow that. He orders you to love your wife with all her defects, except in case of adultery" (*Laus Maximi*, PG 51, 227). An important text also occurs in *In Mattheum Homilia*, XVII, 4; PG 57, 259-260: "Jesus also lightened the law in another way. He gave the husband a resort to repudiation with the words 'except for fornication.'"

[44] *In Matthaeum*, 19, 1-12. PG 36, 291.

"I do not approve this law and I do not praise this custom. It is easy to see that this law was drafted by men, and that they framed it against women."[45]

Equality of men and women before the law, which Christian teachers espoused from time to time, would entail a very serious consequence. The concession of repudiation on the ground of adultery would have to be extended to the wife also. Some bishops in the third century were already applying the rule in that sense, but—as already noted—Origen did not quite approve. Toward the end of the fourth century, on the contrary, Epiphanius was presenting this as the accepted teaching. Here is what he has to say about remarriage.

"He who cannot keep continence after the death of his first wife, or who has separated from his wife for a valid motive, as fornication, adultery, or another misdeed, if he takes another wife, or if the wife takes another husband, the divine word does not condemn him nor exclude him from the Church or the life; but she tolerates it rather on account of his weakness. Not that this man can keep with him two wives, the first one still gravitating around him; but if he is actually separated from his first wife, he may take another according to the law, if this is his desire."[46]

The most important testimony for this decisive period stretching from Nicea to Justinian is Basil (4th century), whose collection of canon laws was accepted as authoritative in both the East and the West. These canons, prepared in answer to questions asked by his friend, Bishop Anphiloquius, provide solutions for the issues of marriage and divorce in terms of the eight different possible situations envisaged in the table set out earlier in this chapter. They establish clearly that patristic teaching on the indissolubility of marriage and the exceptions to that rule is not unitary and monolithic, and that it can be understood by distinguishing various subjects and circumstances.[47]

a) *Innocent husband, separation on ground of adultery.* He

---

[45] *Ibid.*, PG 289.
[46] Panarion, *Haer.*, 59, 4–5. PG 41, 1024.
[47] The canonical letters to Anphiloquius are found in PG 32, col. 677ff (Letter 188), col. 722ff (Letter 199), and col. 804ff (Letter 217).

can remarry (Canon 9). The issue is so clear that Basil does not refer to it directly.[48]

b) *Innocent husband, separation for reason other than adultery.* If he remarries, he is deserving of pardon.[49]

c) *Guilty husband, separation on ground of adultery.* If he remarries after his wife has left him, he is excusable.[50] If, on the contrary, he left his wife in order to remarry, he is an adulterer, but ecclesiastical custom forgives him after seven years of doing penance.[51]

d) *Guilty husband, separation for reason other than adultery.* As in the previous case, if he is abandoned and remarries, he is excusable.[52]

e) *Innocent wife, separation on ground of adultery.* She may not leave her husband; if she does leave him and remarries, she is an adulteress. If her husband leaves her, the case is dealt with in the same way as the following one.[53]

f) *Innocent wife, separation for reason other than adultery.*

[48] "The (adulterous) husband who was abandoned, it can be excused (if he remarries)." The innocent husband does not need any excuse. See Canon 77 quoted in Note 51 below.

[49] Canon 35: "In the case of a husband who has been abandoned, it will be necessary to examine the cause for the desertion. If it is manifest that the woman left without justification, the husband is worthy of forgiveness, and the woman deserves punishment." It is clear that the issue here is abandonment by a wife who has not committed adultery and remarriage of the abandoned husband. Otherwise, he would not need pardon. See also canon 46.

[50] Canon 9 (see also Note 48 above). Here is the stated reason for this extraordinary concession: "The custom also orders adulterous men and those who are in the state of fornicators not to forsake their wives. This is why, if one of these was abandoned (by his spouse), I do not say that one can treat as an adulteress the woman who afterwards marries him. Indeed, the culpable one is here the wife, who has deserted her husband."

[51] Canon 77: "He who has deserted a woman with whom he was lawfully united in order to take another is certainly subject to condemnation as an adulterer in virtue of the sentence of the Lord; but it was decided by our fathers that the culpable ones shall do penance." To judge by this text alone, there is here question of a practice far removed from the Christian ideal. Probably other circumstances are assumed to exist.

[52] This is a deduction from the laxity of the solution provided in the previous case. If remarriage of an abandoned adulterous husband is tolerated, with far more reason must that of one who is less guilty.

[53] Canon 9: "The wife who has abandoned her (adulterous) husband commits adultery if she unites with another man."

If her husband leaves her, the case is a doubtful one, but there would seem to be tolerance.[54]

g) *Guilty wife, separation on ground of adultery.* No concession is admitted, and she is to be repudiated as an adulteress.[55]

h) *Guilty wife, separation for reason other than adultery.* No concession is admitted.

The first point to note is that the concessions in all these cases are granted by way of tolerance. They are considered as in conflict with the ideal of Christian perfection, but they are not less lawful for that reason. Canon 4 sets out the penances to be imposed on those who remarry.

Still more interesting is Basil's attitude toward the glaring inequality of rights of the husband and the wife. As a theologian, he disapproves,[56] but in his canons he limits himself to echoing the Church's practice "received from the Fathers." That practice extends tolerance to almost anything the man may do, and to almost nothing the woman may do.

It is fully proper to ask why Basil accepts a practice opposed to or different from his own theological convictions. The answer is given by the voice of tradition. It is that there is a yet deeper tradition, that of God's condescension, the tradition that caused Origen to write the lofty comments (mentioned above) on St. Matthew's gospel. The moral equilibrium established by the Christian communities when they were small minorities survived in the spirit of the great theologians of the Church after it had achieved majority status. Like Clement of Rome, Tertullian, Clement of Alexandria and Origen, the Fathers of the Byzantine East know that some laws were promulgated in recognition of the weakness of the flesh.

---

[54] Canon 48: "The wife who was abandoned by her husband ought in my view remain alone." Basil does not seem to be sure. One may recall the discretion of Origen when he excused the bishops who authorized a woman in these circumstances to remarry. The *Constitutiones apostolicae* (III, 1, 2) *praise* the young woman who in this case does not remarry.

[55] Canon 21: See canon 8 of Neocaesarea (Pitra, I, 452) and canon 65 of Elvira.

[56] Canon 9: "The declaration of the Lord, that it is not permitted to separate a marriage except for the cause of fornication applies equally to men as to women, if one considers the logical consequence of the idea. However, the custom is different, and we find many more demands imposed upon women." See Canon 21.

Some recent authors seem to suggest that the exceptions allowed to the law of indissolubility merely express pastoral tolerance affecting individuals and are not true exceptions to the law. Their position would be that the Fathers upheld absolute indissolubility while tolerating excusable offenders in the community and admitting them to Communion. This interpretation is not completely correct. In the case of the spouse abandoned on the ground of adultery, the tolerance in favor of the innocent party affected the law and not merely the individuals. The innocent spouse could remarry lawfully, although such a marriage—like that of a surviving spouse—was discouraged pastorally. Illegitimate unions, such as that mentioned by Basil in canon 77, fall into a different category. A man who left his lawful wife and married another was admitted with his new wife to Communion after doing penance for seven years (the penance of one guilty of fornication). Such a union could be classed only as concubinage in Church law. Since, however, civil law permitted the legitimation of such a marriage, the Church tolerated the fact pastorally and admitted the parties to Communion after they had done penance.

It is accordingly important to distinguish the two levels of tolerance with extreme care. Some exceptions to the law were foreseen and provided for by the legislator, while there were other irregular situations not provided for in the law but dealt with by the maternal instincts of the Church. The source of both is the same, namely, God's condescension. But the application and the consequences are different.[57]

From the sixth century onwards, one finds a progressive accommodation of the divorce laws of the Eastern Church to the provisions of Justinian's new code promulgated in 542. Grounds for divorce are widened, and the wife is placed on exactly the same level as the husband. The theological reaction is ambivalent. Some theologians attempt a broad interpretation of the text of St. Matthew to bring other grounds under adultery.

[57] Other interesting testimonies of the Eastern Church in the 4th and 5th centuries (Cyril of Alexandria, Theodoretus, Victor of Antioch) are not reproduced here in the interest of brevity. See Pospishil, *Divorce and Remarriage* (New York: Herder & Herder, 1967), pp. 155ff, and J.B.M. Mayaud, *L'indissolubilité du mariage. Etude historico-canonique* pp. 72ff.

Others, even in the Greek-Slav period, continue to uphold the traditional view that adultery is the only lawful ground. A detailed survey of these positions is not necessary here.[58] It suffices to note that the new collections of Church canons known as the Nomocanon (ninth century) incorporates the Justinian rules in their entirety. While the current legislation of the various Eastern Churches differs considerably, all of them admit more than one ground for divorce.[59]

IV. The West After the Peace of Constantine

The equilibrium of doctrines and moral rules which characterized the period preceding Nicea continued in the West for a long time after the Peace of Constantine, in spite of the fact that it was challenged by even more serious (and quite different) problems than those experienced in the East. During the fourth and fifth centuries, a strong theological tradition retained the formulations regarding indissolubility and the exceptions thereto without change. Side by side with this majority view, however, there arose an intransigent position for the first time. It was backed by the most influential theologians and adopted by the Roman see, thence to be gradually extended throughout the entire area of Latin influence by an instrument of leveling impact, the institution of monasticism. The practice of the Church continued to adjust itself for many centuries to the traditional position, though with swings of the pendulum. It was not until the start of the second millenium that the Cluny reform and the foundation of schools of philosophy influenced by St. Augustine placed what is still the discipline regarding indissolubility of marriage on a firm basis. The various steps must be described in some detail.

The Latin writers who continue the pre-Nicene viewpoints can be passed over quickly. It is enough to quote what they say and leave to the reader the task of interpreting them in accordance with the norms given earlier in this chapter. The theme and content remain constant. Christian marriage, unlike pagan

---

[58] See Jugie's article, "Mariage dans l'Eglise gréco-russe" in *Dictionnaire de Théologie Catholique* (hereafter D.T.C.), vol. 9. col, 2327.

[59] For example, 21 in the Byzantine Church, 10 in that of Russia.

marriage, is indissoluble because God has so decreed. Repudiation is a license contrary to Christian moral teaching, except for a wife' adultery. It has become commonplace to compare the law of the gospel and that of Moses. Hilary of Potiers recalls in the fourth century that, in contrast with the laxity of the Old Testament, the gospel precept forbids the granting of a certificate of divorce "by prescribing no other ground for terminating the marriage beside that which would defile a man because of association with a prostitute wife."[60] And if someone still objects that Hilary speaks only of repudiation and not of remarriage, the answer is—as before—that the repudiation here at issue is repudiation under the Mosaic dispensation and the civil law, both of which authorized remarriage.

Lactantius, a teacher of rhetoric converted to Christianity and a contemporary of Hilary, is even more explicit. "He is an adulterer who married a wife dismissed by her husband, and he who dismissed a wife, except for the crime of adultery, in order to take another woman."[61] Those who deny that Lactantius here authorizes remarriage have to interpret him as saying: "The man who repudiates his adulterous wife and remains unmarried, is not an adulterer." That is equivalent to saying that one who does not commit adultery is not an adulterer.

An identical reference to the prohibition of repudiating one's wife and remarrying, with mention of the exception in the case of the wife's adultery, is found toward the end of the fourth century in Cromacius of Aquileia.[62] This is a very important testimony, because Cromacius was a contemporary of St. Jerome and corresponded with him. Jerome, as will be seen later, forbids remarriage under any circumstances.

Aquileia, the modern L'Aquila, was only a few short miles from Rome. While Bishop Cromacius was expressing the just quoted views, Pope Innocent I was answering questions by applying the same traditional rules. Here are the three principles he proclaimed. 1. Christian moral principles exclude repudiation. 2. There is no exception to this rule in favor of the wife. 3. There

---

[60] *In Matthaeum Commentarium*, 22. PL 9, 939.
[61] *Divinae Institutiones*, VI, 23, 33. PL 6, 720.
[62] *Homilia in Matthaeum*, 19. PL 20, 351.

is an exception in favor of the husband when the wife is guilty of adultery.[63]

The most explicit and unambiguous text of all comes from an unknown author who wrote a commentary in the fourth century on St. Paul's first letter to the Corinthians. St. Ambrose of Milan was believed for many centuries to have been the author of this commentary. According to the unknown theologian, "a man is permitted to remarry if he has dismissed his sinning wife, because he is not limited in his rights as the woman is; after all, the head of the woman is the man."[64] Nor can this author be dismissed as lax. On the contrary, the rest of his commentary is strict and highly traditional, with few new insights.

St. Jerome is the first who tries to put an end to the practice of indulgence, a fact that need cause no surprise. The teaching of this fiery and intransigent man regarding marriage does honor neither to the Church nor to religion. He brings together the most debatable of Tertullian's arguments and expands them in his *Adversus Jovinianum*, a treatise written in Palestine in 393. The work is a pitiful diatribe against marriage, and even Jerome later expressed regret for having written it. It says for example, that "this good of marriage, which is good only because it is a lesser evil, is still suspicious in my eyes."[65] And at least by inference, it brands as an adulterer the man who loves his wife too ardently. According to Jerome, "the wise man should love his wife with his reason, not with his emotions."[66] He felt it necessary to attack marriage in order to promote celibacy. In consequence, one can expect no concession in regard to divorce from him. Following custom and the strict interpretation of the

---

[63] Innocentius I (401–407), *Ad Exuperium*, PL 20, 400; *Ad Victricium*, PL 20, 479; *Ad Probum:* "Marriage with the second woman can in no way be legitimate if the former wife is alive and if she has not been ejected because of divorce" (PL 20, 602).

[64] Ambrosiaster, *In 1 Cor* 7:10–11, PL 17, 218. Modern opponents of divorce cannot downgrade the testimony of this unknown writer unduly, because he happens to be the only ancient witness to the use of the Pauline Privilege. The immediately preceding testimony comes from the 7th century (Theodore of Canterbury), but it also allows the exception on the ground of adultery.

[65] *Adversus Jovinianum* I, 9. PL 23, 233.

[66] *Ibid.*, I, 49. PL 23, 293.

gospel provisions, he absolutely ruled out the remarriage of the innocent abandoned wife.[67]

He could not dismiss the situation of the husband who has repudiated an adulterous wife so easily. He tried, nevertheless, to interpret Mt 19:9 in a way that would strip it of all content. It is a most arbitrary interpretation, and it involves a return on the part of its author to the intemperate climate of his treatise *Adversus Jovinianum*, asserting that marriage is "a danger." In this quite unacademic atmosphere he formulates his conclusion: "The husband is ordered to dismiss his wife on condition that he shall not have a second wife during the lifetime of the first."[68]

Much more could be said about St. Jerome's position on this issue. It is enough, however, to note that it clarifies nothing. We already know that Church law forbade remarriage of an innocent abandoned wife. He nowhere says that this law forbids remarriage of the husband. So all we have are the personal views and interpretations of Jerome regarding marriage, and the less said about them, the better.

With St. Augustine we come to a clear watershed. His formulations and explanations provide the guidelines according to which the teaching of the West develops in the following centuries. In his *Commentary on the Sermon on the Mount*, written in 393 before he had become a bishop, he supported and argued in favor of the view that it was not lawful for the innocent party to remarry even in case of adultery. But it is one thing for an ordinary priest to give his interpretation of the scripture and quite another thing for him to impose laws on the community. And if the Church took Augustine's exegesis seriously, it would have to brand as adulterers those who remarried in such circumstances. To protect himself against that possibility, Augustine added a curious comment: "If a wife is repudiated by a husband with whom she wanted to go on living, he certainly commits adultery who marries her, as the Lord said, but it is doubtful that she shares in his crime."[69]

[67] Epist. 55, *Ad Amandum*, PL 26, 562; *Ad Oceanum*, PL 22, 691.
[68] *In Matthaeum Commentarium*, II, 19. PL 26, 140.
[69] *De Sermone Domini in monte*, I, 48. PL 34, 1253. It is important to note that the reference is here to the wife, who in this case was not considered by the community to be an adulteress.

Notwithstanding such reservations, the strictness of the teaching caused a holy man named Polentius to protest. In two letters to Augustine he defended the common view which provided an exception in case of adultery. Augustine, who in the meantime had become a bishop, reaffirmed his view in two books entitled *De coniugiis adulterinis*. After he had done so, nevertheless, he admitted that the question was an obscure one and that he was merely offering his own view.[70] Later, when reviewing the question in his *Retractationes*, he admitted that "he had not found a perfect solution."[71]

If Augustine defends a strict view at the theoretical level, without being able to satisfy his own doubts, he finds it necessary to compromise when faced with a practical situation. He is put to the test by being asked what he would do with a candidate for baptism who had repudiated his adulterous wife and remarried. And this is his answer. "He who dismissed a wife apprehended in adultery and married another wife seems not to deserve to be put on an even footing with those who dismiss and remarry without having adultery as reason. This is so obscure even in the divine revelation itself, whether he who is without doubt allowed to dismiss an adulterous wife is to be held to be an adulterer should he marry another woman, that, in my judgment, anyone who strays commits in this regard only a venial fault."[72] On another occasion, what he does is to reject on the level of theory something that he sees practiced all around him. "However, how can it be that the husband is permitted to marry another woman after he has repudiated an adulterous wife, while the wife is not permitted to marry another man after she has left an adulterous husband? That I cannot see."[73]

The unique value of Augustine's work on marriage is that he creates for the first time a coherent body of teaching concerning the religious value of the institution. In this doctrinal whole, the bond uniting the spouses acquires a special category, no longer merely juridical but "sacramental" in the full sense of that word. The bond signifies the unbreakable union of Christ and the

---

70 *De coniugiis adulterinis*, I, 32. PL 40, 469.
71 *Retractationes*, II, 57. PL 36, 653.
72 *De Fide et Operibus*, 19. PL 40, 221.
73 *De bono coniugii*, 7. PL 40, 378.

Church, and it is in consequence indissoluble. It is something real which survives separation of the spouses. Augustine's conclusion is that only Christian marriage is indissoluble. The natural law does not exclude divorce.[74]

The views of Augustine did not make an immediate impression on Church discipline. Instead, things continued as before. We have, in the acts of local councils or synods, evidence of extreme value concerning the practices of the Churches in the early Middle Ages. A study of the canons of some of these councils reveals the extent of the changes on the subject of divorce during the period.

As early as 314, a council held at Arles advises the husbands of adulterous wives not to remarry.[75] A century later, two councils in North Africa adjust their views to those of Augustine, without explicitly excluding the exception on the ground of adultery. What they do is to set out the common teaching on indissolubility and ask the Emperor to bring the civil law into conformity with it. It would be out of the question for the bishops to ask the Emperor to refuse absolutely to permit remarriage of an innocent party after adultery.[76]

The most striking decree of the fifth century was promulgated by one of the two councils held at Vannes in 461 and 465. "In respect also of those who have deserted their wives, as it is said in the Gospel 'except for fornication,' and have without proving adultery married others, we decree that they are likewise to be barred from communion, lest the sins passed over by our indulgence should attract others to the licentiousness of error." A council held at Agde in the south of France in 506 promulgated a similar canon.[77]

[74] *Ibid.*

[75] "To those who apprehend their wives in adultery, who are young believers, and are (not) prohibited from marrying, if possible the counsel is given that they should not take others as long as their wives are alive, in spite of the fact that the wives are adulterous." The "not" inserted in parentheses is found in the Hérouville codex and is required by the context.

[76] Council of Carthage (407), canon 105. Council of Mileve (416), canon 17.

[77] Concilium Vaneticum, canon 2 (*Corpus Christianorum*, 148, p. 152). Concilium Agathense (*ibid.*). See also canon 26 of the so-called Council of St. Patrick in PL 53, 822.

It is noteworthy that in all these prescriptions the question of remarriage of the husband because of his wife's adultery is never mentioned directly. There was no need to mention it, because the practice was unchallenged. The regulations are concerned only with subsidiary issues created by the difference between ecclesiastical and civil law. The most debated point was whether the wife should enjoy the same rights as the husband. The pastoral tendency was to put them on an equal footing, but the firm opposition of the theologians held back a juridic admission of the wife's right to remarry. Another source of conflict developed through the gradual broadening of the notion of adultery. Infanticide, for example, was a worse crime than adultery, and many argued that it should be treated in the same way. The theologians, however, refused to accept it as a ground for divorce and remarriage. Such conflicts began a process in the West similar to that which has already been described for the East, leading to assimilation of ecclesiastical to civil law. In the West, nevertheless, the process remained partial, illogical and uncertain.

The two Churches were, in fact, going through two extremely different experiences. Eastern Christianity was for the most part under the sole rule of Christian emperors. The Church in the West was fragmented and had to live under very diverse political systems. Up to the time of Charlemagne toward the end of the eighth century, it lacked a sufficiently powerful base to attempt a unification of ecclesiastical discipline. During the seventh and eighth centuries, the local Churches fought as each best could to retain Christian practices or introduce them into new social situations, in conflict with the customs of the barbarian peoples. It is not surprising that the results differed from place to place. Neither is it surprising that the bishops carried more weight than the few theorizers.

The council of Hereford, which brought together the bishops of the Saxon Church under the presidency of Theodore of Canterbury, offers a classic example of the attitude of Catholic bishops in those difficult times as regards divorce, which was recognized by the laws of the Saxon kings. According to its canon 10, "Every priest shall publicly admonish the people to abstain from unlawful marriages, for a lawful marriage can by no means be separated in accordance with the command of the Lord, except by reason of fornication, or except by mutual consent, and this because of the service of God."[78] What is interesting about this canon is that it makes no distinction between the rights of husband and wife.

Theodore, the president of the council, was a Greek, a native of Tarsus. He is believed to be the author of a collection of penitential canons which reflect strikingly the influence of Basil. Regarding the present question, Theodore lays down that "if the wife of anyone commits fornication, it is allowed to dismiss her and to take another; that is, if the husband dismisses his wife because of fornication, and she was his first wife, he is permitted to take another wife; while she, if she agrees to do penance for her sins, may take another man after five years."[79] The approval of remarriage of the guilty wife reflects a surprising laxity. Other rules in this guide for confessors allow similar kinds of tolerance, extending them to cases other than adultery.

In the eighth century, the Church in France and the new Christian communities in Germany enjoyed the benefits of the work of the tireless apostle, Boniface. A constant fighter for the reform of Christian customs, Boniface took part in 744 in a council at Soissons which was also a civil diet. King Pepin presided. Canon 9 of this council reaffirms the traditional law, prohibiting divorce and remarriage except for the wife's adultery.[80]

The councils of Verberie (756) and Compiègne (757) gave so many concessions that later theologians have worked very hard to discredit them. Some have claimed that they were really only civil diets and that they dealt only with incestuous marriages.[81] There is no proof for such a claim. The civil diets were held apart from the meetings of bishops. The *Capitulare Vernense* affirms explicitly that the canonical order was established

---

[78] Concilium Herefordianum (673), canon 10. PL 95, 182.

[79] *Poenitentiale Theodori Cantabrigensis*, XI. PL 99, 933. The Angers formulary has kept formulas for dissolving marriage and remarriage of both parties (*Formularium Angevinense*, PL 87, 851 and 894).

[80] PL 89, 826. See also canon 5 of Concilium Lietinense (765), presided over by Boniface.

[81] See Vacant, D.T.C., col. 491.

in the Frankish kingdom at Verberie and Compiègne.[82] The tone of the canons is completely ecclesiastical, and it must further be recognized that Frankish Christianity had received its reforming impulse from Boniface.

Verberie and Compiègne authorized the husband to remarry if his wife had conspired to kill him, in case of emigration, in case of incestuous adultery by his wife, and if his wife entered a convent.[83] The wife can remarry if her husband commits incestuous adultery, if he becomes a monk, or if he contracts leprosy.[84]

George, Bishop of Ostia, was present as papal legate at Compiègne. Those who claim that George did not approve of some of the "abuses" voted by the French bishops need to be reminded that 25 years earlier Pope Gregory II had agreed to the remarriage of a husband whose wife had become impotent through illness.[85]

The teaching of Augustine on divorce found no echo in the laws of the Western Churches before the eighth century. The traditional exception for the wife's adultery was continued, and in certain parts additional exceptions were introduced without explanation. But if the specific rules proposed by Augustine were not applied, his doctrinal bases became ever more firmly anchored. Two factors played a decisive part in ensuring the diffusion of Augustine's theology. They were the doctrinal work of Pope Gregory the Great (590–604), and the triumph of monasticism in Europe. Gregory the Great made a synthetic adaptation of the theology of Augustine, described by some as a simplification and by others as a caricature.[86] The Augustine-Gregory formulas were spread throughout the West by the monks as part of the social and civilizing role they played during the period. Monasticism introduced into the Christian

---

[82] Hefele-Leclercq. *Histoire des Conciles* III, 917.

[83] Concilium Vermeriense, canons 5, 9, 10. Concilium Compendiense, canon 13, PL 122, 307–309; 140, 824.

[84] Concilium Vermeriense, canons 2, 18. Concilium Compendiense, canons 13, 19.

[85] Gregorius II, *Epistola ad Bonifatium*, PL 89, 525. Canonists become impotent when they try to force an orthodox meaning into this text.

[86] A. Harnack, *Dogmengeschichte*, III, p. 266.

communities its own ideas and way of life. The monastic life itself was presented as the highest Christian ideal. To compensate for the imperfections of lay life and its concessions to the flesh, a solid system of penitential disciplines was introduced. The married life of the layman was regulated down to its slightest details, with a strict application of the warning of Augustine to the married: the one possible justification for bodily union is the desire to procreate.

The rigorism of Augustine and the monks coexisted for several centuries with the traditional pastoral tolerances, to the distress of the Church rulers.[87] The rigorist attitude gradually extended itself, at first without any doctrinal justification, later with the support of the body of doctrine developed on the subject of the marriage bond. Venerable Bede is a rigorist, but he does not dare to appeal to tradition to support his view. Instead, he introduces it with a modest "I believe that. . . ."[88] In the ninth century, Hincmar of Reims rejects the exception based on the wife's adultery, basing himself on the teaching of such Fathers as Augustine, Jerome, and Innocent I.[89]

From the ninth century onwards, local councils began to proclaim the absolute indissolubility of marriages, expressly denying an exception for adultery.[90] There is no doubt that such unanimity was helped by the political reunification under Charlemagne, which gave Rome a tighter control over ecclesiastical discipline. The first pope to reject in fully clear terms the exception for adultery was John VIII in 877.

The triumph of Augustinian theology and the monks was, however, not total until the eleventh century, in part because of the ecclesiastical decadence of the tenth. Pastoral practice continued for three centuries to admit various grounds for divorce

---

[87] Magingaud who was bishop of Würzburg from 753 to 785 and a student of tradition, complains of the diversity among the Fathers on the issue of divorce and asks his colleague Lulius to clear this up for him (PL 96, 825).

[88] Bede, *Commentarium in 1 Cor* 7.

[89] *De divortio Lotarii*, PL 125, 642 and 650ff.

[90] Friul (791), Paris (829), Nantes (875). Nevertheless, the acts of a council held at Rome under Pope Eugene II in 826 include a canon which admits the exception for the wife's adultery, a canon repromulgated in 853 under Leo IV. See *Monumenta Germanicae Historiae, Concilia*, p. 582.

and remarriage. What we have here are carryovers from the earlier practice, and they lasted longer in England and Germany than elsewhere. The existence of such tolerant practices is absolutely clear from the penitential books and formularies which reflect with absolute authenticity the life of the people. Their compilers gathered together everything that was done, or was more or less admitted, without any attempt to eliminate contradictions or incoherent elements. The most important of such collections was made by Burchard, Bishop of Worms in 1025, and it includes various cases of divorce and remarriage.[91]

The Cluny reforms, by giving additional vigor to the monastic institutions, contributed powerfully to the liquidation of the old marriage customs. The schools attached to cathedrals and monasteries renewed the teaching of St. Augustine, creating a sacramental theology which provided a theoretical foundation for the teaching on the absolute indissolubility of marriage. The universities completed this work from the twelfth century onwards, subsequent theologians repeating unanimously that the unbroken tradition of the Fathers of the Church had denied that adultery was a ground for remarriage following repudiation.

In the above exposition, frequent reference was made to the "pre-Nicene equilibrium." It should be made clear that it was a less than ideal equilibrium, being based on a conformism alien to today's way of thinking. The fact is that the uniformity of viewpoints on divorce up to the fourth century rested on acceptance of an inequality of rights of husband and wife. Christian writers at that time held that the scriptures had established the inequality, and in consequence they accepted it without question.

Such a situation could not long survive the Peace of Constantine. The principle of legal inferiority of the woman in marriage clashed with the Christian moral view, which insisted on woman's dignity. In addition, it became clear that it was illogical to recognize adultery as the only ground for divorce. Such a stand was not adapted to the social situation, in which far worse marriage problems existed. The literal and strict inter-

---

[91] *De Poenitentia*, Book 12. PL 140, 959–966. See also cols. 824 and 826 in this same source.

pretation of scripture could not then be sustained, and in fact it was not.

Two interpretations were offered to resolve the problem. One was that Jesus and Paul mentioned the exception in favor of the husband, not to establish an exclusive rule, but merely as an example. This exegesis, which would allow other grounds at the discretion of the Church, was adopted by most Easterns, implicitly at first and later explicitly. The second interpretation was that Jesus and Paul rejected divorce and remarriage for adultery, allowing a mere separation of the parties. First presented by Jerome and Augustine, it became the official stand of the Western Church from the twelfth century onward.

Two diametrically opposed ways were thus found to reach a new equilibrium. The East gave the woman the same rights as the man. The West denied to the man the rights denied to the woman.[92] And yet there is "one Lord, one faith and one baptism." Which is the God of the innocent spouse in a time of suffering? Is he the condescending God of the East or the intransigent God of the West?

V. RETURN TO TRADITION PROVIDES NO SOLUTION

The study of the patristic texts on divorce and remarriage establishes that they provide no solution. As the theology manuals say, "when the Fathers disagree, their authority does not make a solid argument."

To determine when an argument based on the authority of the Fathers of the Church is solid is one of the most complicated tasks in theology. Rahner-Vorgrimler define a "consensus" of the Fathers as follows: "One must assume agreement when it is possible to prove its existence in all those Fathers who defend a teaching as explicitly revealed, without finding any opposition to their view."[93] On the issue of divorce, we have found not a single Greek Father to hold absolute indissolubility as a teaching of the

---

[92] The gap between the two solutions is reflected in these two decisions. Gregory Nazianzen (PG 36, 289): "I do not approve a law which binds the wife and is indulgent to the husband." Jerome (PL 22, 691): "Between ourselves, what is not allowed to wives is not allowed to husbands."

[93] K. Rahner and H. Vorgrimler, "Consensus," in *Dictionary of Theology* (New York: Herder & Herder, 1966).

faith, nor a single Latin Father before the ninth century. Jerome and Augustine were both very much aware that theirs was a new point of view, and several centuries passed before it gained acceptance.

What is certain is that the treatment of the problem of divorce by the Fathers is unequal, ambiguous and far from logical. The one constant line is the very modest claim that traditional pastoral practice allowed divorce and remarriage of the husband whose wife had committed adultery. The unsuccessful opposition of some Latin Fathers serves only to increase the value as evidence of this universal conviction. But the contribution of this traditional practice of the first thousand years of Christianity to the contemporary problem of divorce is slight, because the very same tradition closes the door against the needed broadening of the toleration to the woman in similar circumstances and to other even graver grounds. Although such extension of the principle was at times authorized, it was done with little or no theological justification, and such efforts were denounced by some authorities as abuses.

A doctrine based simply on the marriage discipline of the first ten centuries would lack the logical cohesion to justify an ecclesiastical practice on the basis of tradition. The general principle that indissolubility permits exceptions was agreed. But its application was partial and inequitable, because of reliance on other moral principles of doubtfully Christian character as the controlling elements in reaching decisions. Some of the background of this doctrinal eclecticism was reviewed early in this chapter. Encratism, with its negative attitude to human sexuality, is the most constant component of the Christian writers studied. Open or implied, strict or moderate, it is always present in some form. Everything associated with the flesh is regarded with suspicion. Marriage is accepted and even defended against such heretical extremists as the Gnostics, Montanists and Manicheans, but a clear dichotomy is at work in the view held by the Christians themselves. The principal value they see in Christian marriage is the spiritual community of the baptized, with the union of bodies regarded as merely to be tolerated, its only justification being the wish to produce new life.

Admittedly, the most representative Fathers defend the rights of the weakest Christians on the basis of the divine condescendence. But the establishment of a category of the imperfect or carnal, the quasi institutionalization of "weakness" inside the Church, clearly indicates an anthropology owing more to Plato than to the Bible. The believer without a vocation to virginity is automatically transferred to a lower category, and the only way he can lift himself back up is by continence as a married man or a widower. In concrete terms, if a man was restored to the single state by the death of his wife or by divorce, this was seen as an opportunity for him to pass to the state of perfection. To remarry, on the contrary, was evidence of a deplorable weakness little different from that of the bigamist unable to control his base passions. Remarriage was tolerated and recognized by the law, but the moral judgment passed on it was strongly influenced by the Gnostic notion of perfection.

In order to avoid the charge of anachronism, theological judgments on the doctrine on marriage of early Christianity taken as a whole have been avoided throughout. The influences of Gnosticism and encratism in various writers have been pointed out, not to pass a theoretical judgment on them, but to present the historical facts. Traditional teaching does, however, hold values for the present in Catholic theology. The modern writer is expected to take the views of other ages into account when attempting theoretic or practical formulations for his contemporaries. In consequence, it is now quite proper to pass the views of the Fathers through the sieve of today's doctrinal context, especially to the extent that those views are final. In a word, the teaching of the ancients can be judged in the framework of our modern categories.

Application of this criteriology to our problem provides the final and conclusive answer concerning the value of the testimony of tradition for the issue under discussion. To begin, the theory and practice of the Fathers were based on a situation which has long disappeared, a situation which encouraged them to transform the Christian rules into a code of laws binding on the whole society. Today's believer turns to the sources of the faith to obtain guidance according to the norms of the gospel and not to find criteria for his judgments regarding human and social well-being. In such a context, he finds in the Christian tradition on divorce a hopeless mixture of divine and human elements. And even if he succeeds in separating the two areas, he is still up against the wall of the total conflict between the two moral viewpoints. There is no escaping the fact that our world cannot accept the sexual anthropology of early Christianity. Its basic assumptions are in conflict with the values placed today, in both human and Christian terms, on the sex function. It is not possible in our days to cast the least moral or religious shadow on the institution of marriage, nor can an arbitrary scale of values be invoked for the purpose of breaking the unity and the complementary character of the bonds joining the spouses. Still less can the opportunities provided by the married state to achieve Christian perfection be questioned. If then we cannot accept the principles, neither can we accept the consequences, namely, the excessive restrictions in the area of marriage legislation. As is now clear, the laws governing marriage flowed organically from the total understanding of human sexuality as seen in religious and moral terms. In consequence, they lack sufficient proof of their doctrinal purity to merit incorporation in a modern Christian anthropology. The Christian answer to contemporary marriage problems needs a higher moral foundation.

The results of the study of the first ten centuries of Christianity can be summed up briefly.

1. Theologians and historians of dogma have failed to take adequately into account the circumstances which constitute the proximate and the remote contexts of the testimonies of tradition.

2. The second and third centuries are characterized by a simple and peaceful acceptance of the scripture provisions understood in their literal sense. In consequence, an innocent husband was allowed to remarry, and an innocent wife was not.

3. The pressure of new social needs in the East forced a broadening of the area of tolerance on the divorce discipline, but without changing the previous theological framework.

4. Social conditions in the West, and especially the predominant influence of monasticism, made possible the diffusion and

establishment of the rigorous opinion of St. Augustine. It was accepted finally as the traditional view.

5. The conflicting views of the Fathers of the Church make it impossible to regard absolute indissolubility of marriage, even in case of adultery, as a truth pertaining to the faith.

6. The social, anthropological and moral context which determined the early Christian discipline regarding marriage and divorce prevent the traditional position from being taken as the starting point for a coherent Christian view of marriage and its social regulation.

7. If the results of this historical study are compared with the conclusions of the previous chapter on the teaching of scripture, it will be seen that both the East and the West departed from the spirit of the gospel when they transformed evangelical rules into binding legislation. The error of the Easterns was to give ecclesiastical approval to something so unChristian as the breakdown of the marriage union; that of the Westerns, to declare immoral something so human as this same breakdown.

CHAPTER 5

The Theology of Marriage

Catholic teaching on marriage is currently being subjected to severe internal and external pressures which threaten to disintegrate its monolithic structure. Of all the points of contact between the Church and the world, marriage is actually the most delicate. It tends, in consequence, to register the slightest change on either slope of its complex socio-religious reality. Humanity, for its part, is today in a new period of its history, a period characterized by profound and rapid changes which are gradually expanding to affect the entire universe. Man himself by means of his intelligence and his creative activity inaugurates the changes, but they soon exert in turn their impact on him, affecting his judgments, his individual and collective desires, his way of thinking, his attitudes toward the reality with which he is in contact, his conduct toward his fellows. This climate of change has progressed to the point where one can speak of a true social and cultural metamorphosis, with significant impact in the area of religion also. History itself is experiencing a process of acceleration of an order that man can scarcely keep up with. Mankind has ceased to have a series of parallel histories and is swept up into a single destiny and fate. It is thus moving from a primarily static conception of reality to a more dynamic and evolutionary one, creating a new set of problems which call for new analyses and new syntheses.

Within such a context, marriage is the Christian institution with the most clearly defined history. Of all the sacraments, it is the one which has developed most through the centuries. In actual fact, it was only in the last century that Catholic teaching on marriage was fully systematized, when the last surviving elements of Gallicanism were liquidated. One could almost say that marriage reached its fullness just as it was caught up in crisis.

In any case, under the impact of the deep changes wrought in society, the crisis arrived. The process of desacralization, of secularization, is not only irreversible but has already penetrated all the sanctuaries hitherto reserved to religious influences, while the walls of "the City of God" have been razed and it has grown together with the city of men. The Christian becomes steadily more reluctant to accept social and religious laws born under the sign of a medieval Christianity and set up by the Catholic ghetto of the Counter-Reformation as the mark and measure of religious orthodoxy. Theology has rediscovered the personal dimension of the Christian's vocation, causing those who still talk to God to reject unnecessary intermediaries. The sacraments—including the great sacrament, the Church itself—are no longer regarded as roads, stairways or walls between man and God, but as places of encounter. And for this function we have far too many laws, regulations, rites and institutions, but not nearly enough testimonies and prophets. However naive, such is the language which Christian thinkers of today use and many Christians of today understand. A living community of men in dialogue with the world and desirous of giving a spiritual testimony to the world must of necessity soon find itself on a collison course with the doctrinal and legal rigidities of Catholic marriage legislation. Christians want nowadays to be honest with God and with their fellow men. The place where they must inescapably begin is at the point of their insertion as living humans in the homeland of the world, marriage and the family.

This chapter studies official Catholic teaching on divorce, showing how it has evolved historically. The first part will include rather informal comments on each of the basic elements used to build the classic theology. Then will come an historical synthesis seeking to extract from the mass of data the principal ideas and tensions which produced the present situation. Such a global survey must precede the presentation of a specific proposal concerning remarriage of an abandoned spouse, because this problem, far from being an isolated one, is intimately related to all other marriage issues. Simply to propose a particular type of renewal of one aspect of discipline would run the risk of mending an old dress with new cloth, with easily foreseeable results. The need for a completely new dress has to be shown, and while more competent tailors are being sought, an idea of the size and nature of the task can be indicated.

I. THE DOCTRINAL ELEMENTS

Five aspects of the Catholic doctrinal system governing marriage have to be distinguished. First comes a question of public law of transcendent social importance, the Church's power over marriage. Next are two closely connected theological points, the identity of contract and sacrament, and the notion of the sacramental bond. That leaves two matters concerning divorce, the natural indissolubility of marriage, and the absolute indissolubility of a consummated marriage between Christians.

1. *The Church's power over marriage*

Canon 1016 states that marriage between baptized persons is governed by both the divine law and canon law. This is an assertion that power over such marriages belongs to the Church, a claim based on the teaching about marriage as a sacrament. The sacred character of such marriages causes them to come within the competence of the Church, a competence finally asserted as exclusive.

Such a position, nevertheless, is quite recent. Before the creation of a politico-ecclesiastical theocracy in Western Europe, Christians regulated their matrimonial relations in accordance with the civil law, the Church limiting itself to telling them what conditions they were bound in conscience to fulfill in order to ensure that this civil and human action was invested with Christian religious value. The political and social chaos of the ninth to eleventh centuries placed in the hands of the Church the instruments of power to regulate all aspects of the institution of marriage. Justification was established quickly after the fact. In a marriage of Christians, went the thesis, civil authority has competence merely as regards the secondary and purely civil effects

of the contract. Such a claim represents a flagrant demand of
worldly privileges on the part of the Church. It effectively re-
serves the exclusive power to determine all the conditions a marriage must fulfill in order to be valid, denying such power not
only to all Catholic states but to any state which has Christian
citizens.

Even if we agree that a sacred entity called "the sacrament of
matrimony" exists, this stand is illogical. The existence of a sacred
element would authorize the Church to determine the conditions
for the validity of that element, but it would offer no justification for interfering in the juridic and social aspects of marriage.
Within the community of believers the Church can freely create
its own juridic system, to be urged exclusively in the forum of
conscience. What it cannot properly do is to create binding rules
affecting social life, an activity which would go completely beyond its mission of prophecy and witness.

In this framework, it makes no sense for one of the communities to which the spouses belong to rule on the legal status of
the marriage in the other. As was said earlier, the Roman Catholic
Church has claimed for some centuries the right to deny any
value whatever to the civil regulation of marriage contracted by
two members of the Catholic community. This extremist doctrine
lacks any solid backing in tradition. The first pope to assert exclusive Church jurisdiction over marriage was Pius VI, who in
1788 gave a strict interpretation of Trent's canon 12, which in
fact merely repeated the common and obvious teaching that the
Church has power in marriage cases. The proposed basis for this
claim of exclusivity is the teaching on the identity of contract and
sacrament. If the sacrament is the contract itself, the whole comes
under the Church's sole control.

This view leads in the contemporary world to extremely radical
consequences. The Church teaches that the family is the basic
cell of society, while simultaneously withdrawing the social ordering of the family from the authority of the state. In addition,
the claim assumes a system of union of church and state, or at
least a situation of very special privilege for the Catholic Church.

A state that fully accepts the Church's claim on this matter is
forced to convert its marriage legislation into a source of inter-

national disorder in an area which is already poorly organized. For example, in a country in which only canonical marriage is accepted as civilly valid, the Church officials rule invalid all marriages between Catholics contracted civilly in other countries and agree to marry anyone who can show that he has not contracted a canonical marriage. The result is to permit marriages so blatantly immoral that the countries with the most liberal divorce laws would forbid them. The candidate for bigamy need not even take the trouble of a divorce when he can have his wife ruled a concubine by the Church. This kind of thing actually happens in Spain and Italy.[1]

The theory of the exclusive right of the Church over the marriages of baptized persons has created the most absurd situations for several centuries. The decree *Tametsi* of the Council of Trent required the presence of the pastor or his delegate for validity of a marriage. Trent's decrees were not promulgated in England and in most of the United States, but they were promulgated in most of Europe, and the Church ruled in consequence that marriages of Protestants were there invalid through "defect of form." The first break did not come in this incredible ruling that millions of good Germans and Dutch were living in concubinage until 1741, when Benedict XIV provided an exemption for situations in which non-Catholics and Catholics lived side by side. Restricted at first to the Low Countries, this exemption was gradually extended elsewhere. A general exclusion of Protestants from the canonical form was, however, not given until Pius X's *Ne temere* issued in 1907, with effect from April 1908. That was three and a half centuries after Trent.

To the inconsistency of the theological foundation and to the practical problems that result from it must be added another significant factor. The Church's hierarchy no longer attempts to assert this claimed right and speaks less and less about its existence. The documents of Vatican Council II completely ignore it,

---

[1] W. Bertrams states that "in many countries" the Church does not admit to canonical marriage those bound by a civil marriage ("De influxu Ecclesiae in iure baptizatorum" in *Periodica de re morali, canonica et liturgica*, 49 (1960), p. 448). This is a praiseworthy initiative based in common sense but not directly approved by canon law.

in spite of their explicit references to marriage and the civil power.[2] Nowadays the Church everywhere accepts the competence of the state in regard to the public ordering of marriage, demanding for itself only the same facilities as accorded to other religious bodies.

Father L. C. M. Meyers, a Dutch canonist, recently pointed out the disadvantages of a juridic regulation of marriage by the Church. "Judgments about marriage in so far as it is an earthly reality are matters for the civil juridic order in the first instance," he says in the course of an explanation of how the Church historically became involved. "The Church intervened in this field because the civil authority was breaking down. Nevertheless, the acts of the Council of Trent show that a far from insignificant minority of the Fathers judged that the Church's intervention at that time was an unlawful interference in the life of society. Besides, the function which the Church believed it could exercise at that time has long since been taken back by the civil authority. In spite of this, the Church still maintains its own system of legal rules, in part because of the sclerosis which affects in time every juridic system, and in part because of the Church's carryover from its medieval past of a tendency to think of itself as a kind of state."[3]

Basic to the whole of this way of formulating the issue is the theological distortion which occurred during the Constantine period, transforming into a juridic obligation what should be presented simply as a moral norm. By claiming the right to impose a Christian legislative system on the whole of society, the Church found itself in the position of having to present as legal canons the moral precepts which ruled entry into and membership of the Christian community, acts which of their nature represent an exercise of free will.

[2] Referring to marriage and the family, Vatican II's *Pastoral Constitution on the Church in the Modern World* says (Par. 52): "Public authority should regard it as a sacred duty to recognize, protect, and promote their authentic nature, to shield public morality, and to favor the prosperity of domestic life."

[3] In an interview with the daily *De Volkskrant*, June 25, 1966; reproduced in *Informations Catholiques Internationales*, 268 (1966), pp. 26–27.

The ecclesiastical juridic regulation of marriage thus inescapably becomes an "ersatz" of the gospel, with results easily observable by anyone who as a sociologist studies the life of the countries which are still affected.

One final observation is pertinent. During the period of anticlerical governments in Europe and Latin America, "civil marriage" was always a key issue. What the secularists did in this instance was simply to take over marriage in the precise terms in which the Church had formulated it and transfer the ceremony from the sanctuary to the town hall. They claimed, but quite wrongly, that the state was taking back a function which the Church had usurped. The civil authorities had not at an earlier period exercised or claimed a direct control over the form in which marriage was contracted, and consequently they could not take back what they never had. Marriage is an agreement between two persons, and all that pertains to civil society is to take note of it when it occurs. It is the right of every person to join in marriage with whom he will and how he will. The state can only establish conditions under which it will regard that union as lawful for all purposes.

One such condition may be that the parties have to appear before a judge and two witnesses, but such an appearance does not make the marriage. All it does is to give it standing in the eyes of the civil law. When this personal freedom is clearly re-established, it may be that the Church will one day find that the "privileges" it once claimed will be returned to it. But they will be returned only by those who rightfully possess them, the individuals, and not by society. Only by putting the problem in this personalist perspective can the issue of the age-old conflict between church and state over the marriage of those who owe allegiance to both be solved or declared inexistent. If we start from the principle that the basic competence belongs to the parties, the different spheres and functions can be easily distinguished.

The directions of modern thought and the widespread contemporary practice suggest the following conclusions.

1. The state enjoys the inalienable right to determine the civil legal order of marriage, an order applicable to all citizens without distinction on religious or other grounds.

2. The Church should recognize the right of civil society[4] and instruct its members accordingly as regards the criteria to adopt when judging the impact of concrete situations on the religious values of marriage. The Church is, therefore, entitled to pass judgment on the Christian adequacy of certain marriages without the civil authority being obliged to take its decisions into account.

3. The members of the Christian community accept the civil and public judgment on marriages in their conduct and social relations, while retaining the right to express a different opinion in the religious forum.

4. The Church would be well advised to drop most of its marriage regulations, limiting itself to expressing moral judgments on the different situations to the extent to which they reflect or depart from the Christian ideal regarding marriage. This decision would be particularly important in so far as it would affect the form of marriage. The Church would accept the civil rules and customs, recognizing sacramental value in principle to every marriage of Christians validly contracted according to civil law.

2. *Identity of contract and sacrament*

The Church's claim to competence in regard to the legal ordering of marriage, first established as a fact, was given its doctrinal justification by identifying the contract with the sacrament. This question, consequently, needs to be studied, although it should first be noted that it is speculatively distinct from the one discussed above. What that means is that the legitimacy of civil jurisdiction over marriage is not the starting point to show that a non-sacramental marriage agreement between Catholics is possible. The proof rests on an analysis of the concept of the sacrament of marriage itself.

It is normal for religions to attribute a sacred character to marriage. In the case of Christianity, nevertheless, this was not

---

[4] Such recognition is given de facto in our days. But not a few Catholics still hanker for the old regime. Here is a significant passage from Joyce. He is commenting on the English law of 1898 granting civil effects to religious marriage: "For the Catholic Church the inconveniences are very much the same as where civil marriage is obligatory; for it is always possible for a Catholic to enter on a union which the church assures him has not and cannot possibly have that character" (Op. cit., p. 267).

done easily, and it did not form part of the original nucleus of the Christian tradition. The teaching of Augustine played an important part here. Following its guidelines, the first scholastic theologians succeeded in squeezing marriage into the recently formulated category of the sacraments. Modern Catholic theology starts from the unchallenged premise that marriage is a sacrament. In order to follow the dialectical play of this doctrinal complex more easily, the discussion will start from the same position, though with the important reservation that the sacramental theory is not considered an absolute and definitive theological position, but only a speculative and ultimately deficient expression of the religious values of Christianity. Marriage may provisionally be called a sacrament, until a more modern and freer theology, unfettered by the metaphysical categories of Plato, provides a more adequate definition of its religious values.

The teaching on marriage-as-sacrament can be expressed with an ambiguity that distorts its religious meaning, if it is said that "marriage and the sacrament of matrimony are one and the same thing." The formulation can be and at times is carried even further. Accepting as data of saving revelation views which are no more than the conclusions of theological and juridic speculation, the mystery of Christian marriage is expressed as meaning that "the contract and the sacrament are one and the same thing in a marriage of two baptized persons."

This last formula assumes that the essential constituent of the marriage is the contract, an assertion that results from an extreme interpretation of the aphorism of Roman law that *"consensus, non concubitus, facit nuptias"* (consent, not cohabitation, makes a marriage). Correctly interpreted, this saying means that the presence of the marriage is established by the fact of freely accepted living together, and not precisely by the bodily union. The modern idea, jumping over the legal misunderstandings, has joined up with the sensible and human realism of Roman law.[5] The rich reality of marriage breaks on all sides out of the

[5] This does not mean that the contractual aspect was disregarded in Roman law. Quite the contrary. In Roman society, as in the West up to recent times, marriage presupposed commitments and the establishment of

narrow mold of a contract, and it is this reality—not a single component part—that has been raised to the dignity of a sacrament.

Helped by this striking new formula, the post-Tridentine theologians took the final step. If the contract and the sacrament are identical in marriage, the contract cannot exist unless the sacrament is also present. In consequence, the only valid marriage for the baptized is a sacramental one. If it is not a sacrament, it is not a marriage.[6]

The logic of the conclusion calls for examination. It starts from a traditional and unchallenged statement, namely, that the sacrament of matrimony consists in the marriage itself. However, it changes that statement into a non-traditional and questionable one, namely, that the sacrament consists in the contract. Then it seeks to turn this second statement around by saying that the contract consists in the sacrament, an obvious logical fallacy.[7]

It is necessary to take another look at the social reality of marriage. As already noted, the root from which marriage springs is the voluntary union of the spouses with the intention of establishing a family. This union, "consensus" in the classical Roman sense, constitutes the fact of marriage, a fact with undeniable social and human dimensions. If certain civil conditions are added to the fact, the union will be considered valid in the

---

relationships between the families. In every legal system for marriage, the families of the contracting parties have a decisive importance. This aspect is already to be seen in the first document of the Old Testament to refer to the union of husband and wife: "Therefore a man leaves his father and mother and cleaves to his wife" (Gen 2:24). To recognize this does not reduce marriage to the category of a contract.

[6] Opposition to this thesis ended only with Pope Pius IX. Its great defenders were Bellarmine and Sánchez in the 16th and 17th centuries. They concentrated on attacking the contrary view of Melchior Cano. Vázquez still retained in the 17th century the distinction between contract and sacrament, and the Gallican theologians relied on him when defending the competence of the state in marriage matters.

[7] If the statement, "There is a sacrament," is designated by A; and the statement ,"There is a contract," by B; then we can state: A → B. In no way, however, can the following deduction be drawn: (A → B) → (B→ A). Instead, it is legitimate to conclude that "if there is no contract, there is no sacrament," by applying the *Modus Tollens*: (A→ B) → (−B → −A).

eyes of the civil law, and we have a valid civil contract. If the spouses are Christians and fulfill in addition certain canonical requirements, the union will be a sacrament, a visible sign of the union of Christ and his Church. If it does not fulfill these conditions, the union will be still valid in the purely civil order, an order which exists quite independently of the ecclesiastical. A civilly valid matrimonial union of Christians which is not a sacrament is consequently possible.

If somebody wants to call the civilly valid union "a natural contract," it follows that a natural contract of marriage can exist between Christians without being a sacrament. The terminology, however, does not seem particularly helpful.

To sum up, the doctrine of the identity of contract and sacrament in marriage is an inadequate and ambiguous expression of the mysterious and saving reality of Christian marriage. Its sacramentality is nothing other than the human reality itself presented as an intelligible sign of the divine reality. But that human reality retains its earthly autonomy, and it is the free decision of the Christian which determines whether or not it takes on its divine dimension. What this means is that two baptized persons can contract a valid marriage which is not a sacrament.

3. *The marriage bond*

The notion of contract leads to the notion of bond, understood as the permanent form of the contract. Those who understand marriage as a contract consequently conceive of the bond as expressing its sacramental reality. This places the problems raised in the previous section in a new perspective and calls for reconsidering them.

It is routine theological teaching that the essential effect of a valid matrimonial contract is the bond, and that by its nature the bond is perpetual and exclusive. Indissolubility is thus one property of the bond. At the same time, theologians agree that it is not certain that a natural marriage[8] is absolutely indissolu-

---

[8] "Absolute indissolubility" means an indissolubility that admits of no exception whatever. This expression avoids the distinction between an "intrinsically soluble contract" (which can be broken by the parties themselves) and an "extrinsically soluble contract" (which can only be broken

ble, and the current trend is to challenge the arguments supporting such absolute indissolubility. The fundamental reason for the indissolubility of Christian marriage is, then, its sacramental nature. The marriage union represents the union of Christ with his Church and shares its indissolubility.

This theory, however, seems to raise more issues than it settles. First of all, it has already been noted that it is not enough to define marriage simply as a contract, because this falls far short of exhausting the total reality of the union of the spouses. What makes a marriage is the "consensus" understood as a community of life. It is this consensus that is fully capable of expressing the human values of the marriage and that takes on the additional function of expressing the mystery of Christ and the Church.[9] In this perspective, it has been observed that the search for the saving meaning of marriage should be oriented less toward the properties of the contractual bond than toward the characteristics of the community of life and the mutual self-giving of the spouses. Absolute indissolubility is not the only exemplary aspect of the union of Christ with the Church. On the contrary, this is not even its essential quality as a model. Although Christ and the Church are in fact absolutely inseparable, what is most significant is the depth and totality of their union.[10] In this sense, only a marriage enjoying union can ex-

---

by an outside authority). This terminology stresses unduly the legal aspect of marriage, as in fact does also the term *indissoluble*. "Inseparable," with overtones closer to the human reality of married life, would be a better word.

[9] This presentation gets over the old dispute in the Middle Ages regarding the essential element in the sacrament of matrimony, whether to place it in the contract or in the union of bodies. The scholastics divided into two great currents on the issue. The French, with Peter Lombard, held that the marriage became a reality when the contract was concluded. Gratian, followed by the Bologna school, taught that the marriage did not exist until the union of bodies had occurred. The Italian view gradually lost ground, and with the Decretals of Gregory IX in the 13th century, it was admitted that the consent of the spouses sufficed to create the marriage bond. The view of the School of Bologna, nevertheless, is reflected in the ecclesiastical discipline permitting the dissolution of the bond of a non-consummated marriage.

[10] According to Rahner, the theologically fundamental assertion in Eph 5:29-33 is that the unity of love as such in one flesh and one body constitutes a parallel between Christ-Church and marriage ("Die Ehe als Sakrament" in *Geist und Leben*, 40 (1967), pp. 177-193).

press the saving mystery. Unity is an indispensable property for the existence of the sign. Indissolubility, on the other hand, affects the perfection of the sign but is not essential to its existence. But unity indicates a relationship to the whole of the marriage, while indissolubility looks only to its contractual aspect.[11]

It follows from the above that the meaningful reality in the sacrament of matrimony is the loving union of man and wife, and the reality it evokes is the loving union of Christ and his Church. To introduce new meanings into this simple relationship is to break the transparency and efficacy of the symbolism. That is a lesson in human psychology which is also basic to the advertising art. The message in a good advertisement is always uncluttered.

All the foregoing can be brought together in three points:

1. The loving and stable union of husband and wife, in their worldly and historic condition, is considered religiously suitable to represent to believers the mysterious union of Christ with the Church.[12]

2. The expressive element in the human reality is the community of life of the spouses. Indissolubility, since it is not a constant property of natural marriage, cannot be the primary meaningful element. Nevertheless, the model of Christ and the Church is an illustration for the Christian spouses of the perfectly ideal union as requiring absolute stability.[13]

[11] In the Old Testament, epithalmic images are the ones that most vigorously express the covenant and the election of the people of Israel by God, as in Ezek 16:8–9. New Testament theology knows the category of "covenant," but does not apply it to the relations of Christ with the Church, and consequently not to its symbol, marriage, either. God concludes with men a new covenant mediated by Christ (Heb 8:6–13; Gal 4:21–31), but Christ does not make a covenant with the Church. Rather, he unites himself to it; or more precisely, he unites it to him. The inspired theologians did not regard the notion of "contract" as appropriate for expressing this mystery.

[12] Rahner makes the excellent point that marriage by itself is already a theological sign, with the consequence that Christian theology cannot affirm that the relation between a sacramental and a non-sacramental marriage is the same as that between a sacrament and a profane human act (*Art. cit.*).

[13] Fidelity is a necessary characteristic of the marriage union but is not identified with indissolubility. As Father Duquoc says: "Fidelity is not indissolubility. The authentic encounter demands fidelity. But this does not

3. The attempt to establish a necessary relationship between the indissolubility of the union of Christ with the Church and the indissolubility of the Christian marriage contract tends to present this property as a physical law of the supernatural organism. In actual fact, the indissolubility of the sacramental marriage is a moral law expressing the Christian ideal and giving it proper guidelines. But it must not be regarded on any account as a quasi-physical law, that is to say, a law based on the very essence of the thing. A physical law admits no exception. A moral law calls for exception, if it is to adjust to the needs of the social body whose life it directs.

4. Indissolubility of natural marriage

Marriage just as it is, in all its human reality, is given new religious meaning by Christianity. It is now appropriate to examine whether this human reality includes the property of indissolubility. The previous section indicated that it does not, but the reasons require further development.

First of all, the notion of natural marriage needs to be clarified. It can suggest that a distinct reality known as a supernatural marriage also exists. What it really means, however, is simply a marriage as it presents itself for human examination, leaving aside any additional light that may be available from revelation.

Marriage is a stable relationship, and its stability is threatened by separation and by dissolution. Separation is judged by the fact of marital union. If it has ended, the result is separation. Dissolution is judged by the juridic bond which resulted from the freely accepted union. If the bond disappears, the result is dissolution.

The problem arises when separation and dissolution are established as general principles of separability and dissolubility, and then applied to marriage. Is marriage separable? Is marriage dissoluble? The former question is answered by simply looking at observable facts. Spouses separate and in consequence are in

---

necessarily mean the indissolubility of the bond. Fidelity is a subjective quality of reciprocity. It is difficult to imagine love with fidelity. Indissolubility, on the other hand, is an objective quality of the institution" (*Le Mariage* [66th ed.; Tournai: Mame, 1967], p. 176).

some way separable. The second question bears on a legal issue, and answers vary according to the starting point of the enquirer.

A Catholic tradition with a far from consistent history distinguishes "intrinsic" and "extrinsic" indissolubility,[14] claiming that natural law excludes intrinsic indissolubility but does not in theory absolutely exclude extrinsic. Such is the theory, but in practice Catholic jurists say that exceptions to indissolubility can be granted only by divine right, and concretely only by the pope as the sole depositary of this particular right. To answer their claim requires a change of perspective and the setting up of certain criteria which will eliminate the divergence between the fact and the right, between the separability and the dissolubility of marriage.

The ending of a marriage cannot be viewed exclusively in terms of its juridic and social components. The inadequacy of looking at marriage as merely a contract has already been established, because the reality of the marriage union is far broader than the narrow compass of its juridic concept. The same comments are valid about the ending of the union, a human reality no less complex and delicate.

To consider marriage as a natural social institution enables it to be defined by means of the juridic notion of a contract. The permanence of the contract is the basis for the bond, and the latter is the passive subject of the properties of solubility and indissolubility. But even before it becomes an institution, marriage is a function, the need for which arises directly from the sexual nature of man. This function is defined by the marital union in all its meanings, and the permanent foundation of the union is love. Love establishes the need not to be separated. Marriage, in consequence, tends to be permanent.

Separation has also social effects. In the social context, marriage becomes an institution, and society properly feels the need to safeguard its institutions with appropriate legal prescriptions. Here two elements are pertinent. On the one hand, marriage stability is good for the community. On the other, when the

14 The significance of this distinction was explained in note 8, above.

spouses make their union a contract and accept the civil statute governing marriage, they submit to certain conditions and undertake certain public commitments, including the duty to feed and educate their children. Society, in consequence, has the right to regulate the fulfilment of the marriage commitment, and this right should be exercised by observing the general criteria for the use of every right, namely, by maintaining an equilibrium between the demands of private interests and those of the common good.

Public authority can neither exclude absolutely a breach of the marriage bond, nor can it leave its dissolution to the simple decision of the parties. Society should take into account the basic fact of separation, which breaks the conjugal union and empties the marriage of all human and ethical content. Separation tends spontaneously to become dissolution, or in other words, a de facto situation calls for its juridic recognition.[15] Such recognition should be granted in accordance with rules capable of being revised from time to time in order to protect the interests of the community. To say that no marriage can be legally dissolved is to trample without reason on the rights of the citizens. So universal a law is by its nature contrary to the common good.

There is also another reason why the civil authority should permit marriage to be dissolved by divorce. To live in a community of marriage is a fundamental need of man. The ending of a first cohabitation by separation does not extinguish that need but rather urges the formation of a new union. This is the fact to which society is called to give public recognition. The civil power has the obligation to support this right to the extent which the defense of the common good permits, that is to say, by passing laws permitting divorce and remarriage.

The above explanations call for clarification on two points. First, the notion of the common good is not to be defined in a

---

[15] And purely external. Society has no competence over the union in itself, as G. Crespy explains very well: "Society does not have the right to decide that a conjugal union can be broken. It can certainly establish divorce legislation to deal with cases in which the legal act of marriage can be broken, and the conditions under which the spouses can be freed from their reciprocal legal obligations" (*Le Mariage*, p. 30).

theoretic or a priori way. The common good as applied to the institution of marriage is not established by philosophical, ethical or religious reasoning. It must start with sociological and experimental considerations and therefore be subject to a continuous process of revision and adaptation. In consequence, it is improper to argue against civil divorce starting with philosophic or religious concepts of the family, the state, education and similar matters. Instead, divorce laws should be modified as a result of sociological studies which show their impact on society, for example, when a correlation is established between divorce and juvenile delinquency.

Second, responsibility for the rupture has to be considered. The fact that responsibility was not mentioned earlier does not mean that it has no place in civil legislation on divorce. Separation usually occurs as a result of a transgression or the improper conduct of one spouse, and the law cannot put innocence and guilt on an equal footing. It should protect the innocent and punish the guilty. And even if it is often impossible to determine guilt legally, there is still a place for moral fault and a corresponding sanction in the realm of religion and in the community.

One overall conclusion should now be clear, namely, that marriage can be dissolved under the natural law.[16] This statement will, however, be understood adequately only if it is realized that it is a simple consequence of the previous affirmation of the right to separate. The concept of separation gives divorce the whole of its human dimension, even placing in stronger relief the rift implied in the ending of a marriage union begun through love. While the juridic order cannot be founded on the variations of human emotions, neither can it ignore the practical effects. Marriage, as institutionalized love, disappears when the love runs out. It is pointless to weep over the fickleness of the human heart. Nor is anything to be gained

[16] Häring admits that "in a wounded order the dissolution of a merely natural (non-sacramental) marriage cannot be automatically excluded. For human reason there remains the great difficulty of recognizing that in such cases the regulation (of such dissolution) is reserved to the positive intervention of God" (*Marriage in the Modern World* [Westminster, Md.: The Newman Press, 1965], p. 331).

by using social laws in an effort to educate people. Law cannot have ideals. It should limit itself to organizing as best it can the complex world of the relations of men in society.

5. Indissolubility of consummated sacramental marriage

Working its way through historical reverses, mistaken maneuvers, and strategic detours, the Roman Catholic juridic teaching on marriage has ended up by entrenching itself in a position which it claims cannot be abandoned, the indissolubility of a consummated sacramental marriage. By this is meant a validly contracted marriage between baptized persons ("ratum") which has been completed by the marriage union ("consummatum"). And although nobody has so far tried to proclaim it a dogma of faith,[17] the tendency of the last several centuries has been to regard it as irreversible teaching.

As we noted when reviewing the end of the patristic era, the criterion of absolute indissolubility, even in case of adultery, prevailed at the level of theory by the ninth century, as a result of an explicit return to the teaching of St. Augustine. The collections of canons show that practice remained uncertain for two centuries more, but the Gregorian reform in the eleventh century eliminated the last doubts. The Decree of Yves of Chartres retouched the texts of the councils and the earlier corrections favorable to divorce, thus barring the way with efficient speed to any temptation to return to the older discipline.[18] The Decree of Gratian in the twelfth century established definitely the absolute indissolubility of marriages of baptized persons.

The moral views of St. Augustine and the monks had, however, triumphed before the theological and legal bases had been fully established. The exact definition of marriage and the way to integrate into it the formal aspect of sacrament remained to be determined. Theologians divided on these issues in the twelfth century. Peter Lombard and the French group regarded

---

[17] The Council of Trent explicitly excludes certain grounds for divorce but in order not to alienate certain Eastern Churches further, it does not define absolute indissolubility. See Denzinger, 977. J. Dupont reviews the debates of Trent and explains their meaning in *Mariage et divorce dans l'Evangile*, pp. 115–122.

[18] See Esmein-Genestal, *Le mariage en Droit canonique*, II, p. 88.

marriage as completed by the contract, while Gracian and the Bologna school insisted that there was no marriage without the bodily union. For this reason, the Italians held that a marriage which had been contracted but not consummated could be dissolved. Ecclesiastical practice for a time fluctuated because of these two viewpoints, but finally the Roman Church decided that it could dissolve non-consummated marriages for reasonable cause,[19] while holding consummated marriages to be absolutely indissoluble.

The establishment of a rigorous teaching and practice on indissolubility was helped by the development and systematization of impediments to marriage, leading to the practice of declaring the bond null. The Church of the era of the barbarians urged a strict discipline regarding impediments of consanguinity. Others were gradually added, as can be seen in the rhymed formulas common in the Middle Ages. Diocesan tribunals were authorized to pass judgment in these cases, and a fairly broad interpretation of the impediments eased in practice the strictness of the new law of indissolubility. In addition, the very concept of consummation, capable of being interpreted in many ways, creates a built-in difficulty. The Church law thus found indirect and tortuous ways to satisfy the social need for a legal statute permitting Christians to separate and remarry.[20]

The Protestant Reformation, by breaking decisively with the minor medieval traditions, caused a violent Catholic reaction which froze the process of theological reflection on this issue, as on so many others. The new methods and criteria of biblical exegesis adopted by the humanistic flowering of the Renaissance were no longer permitted to be applied to a question now ruled to be resolved and outside the area of discussion.

Before the Council of Trent, nevertheless, two Catholic theologians, Cardinal Thomas Cajetan (died, 1534) and Bishop Ambrosius Catharinus (died, 1553), both Dominicans, supported an

[19] At first, only one spouse had to join a religious order. Starting in the 15th century the popes broadened the concessions, to the great scandal of the theologians, as stated in Anthoninus of Florence's *Summa Theologica*, III, tit. 1, cap. 21.

[20] See the section on marriage impediments by E. Valton in his article on Marriage in *D. T. C.*, cols. 2440–2449.

interpretation of the phrase of Mt 19:9 favoring divorce on the ground of adultery.[21]

In the years immediately preceding the second Vatican Council, some suggestions were made for changing the canonical formulation of the principle of indissolubility. On the ground that the dissolubility of all classes of marriage is governed by the same law, W. R. O'Connor argued that the pope has the right to dissolve consummated marriages in the same way as those not consummated. He added, however, that the popes could never go back on the decision they had made not to use this right.[22]

Jiménez Urresti believes that the "salus animarum" (salvation of souls), the principle inspiring disciplinary concessions in favor of certain types of divorce, is a social principle in virtue of which "the Church could determine in a future law the cases in which she would by use of her public power dissolve a marriage both ratified and consummated."[23]

A. Bride proposes a new understanding of the concepts of sacramentality and consummation to bring new situations within the present disciplinary framework.[24] García Barriuso follows a similar line.[25]

Archbishop Zoghby's intervention at the Council returned the issue to the dogmatic and pastoral area, in which it had long been ignored. The proposal of the Melchite archbishop of Cairo was received coldly in Roman circles. Cardinal Journet was

---

[21] "I understand from this law of Our Lord Jesus Christ that it is permitted to a Christian man to dismiss a wife because of carnal fornication on the part of his wife, and that he can take another wife, excepting of course definition from the Church which has not yet appeared" (Cardinal Cajetan, *Commentarium in Evangelism secundum Mattheum*, in loc.). "Neither from the Gospel nor from the Apostle can it be deduced that it is not permitted to contract another marriage because of adultery" (Ambrosius Catharinus, *Adnotationes in Commentarium Caietani*, p. 500).

[22] W. R. O'Connor, "The indissolubility of a ratified, consummated marriage" in *Ephemerides Theologicae Lovanienses*, 12 (1936), pp. 692–722.

23. T. J. Jiménez Urresti, *Estudios de Deusto*, 8 (1961), p. 325.

[24] A. Bride, "Le pouvoir du Souverain Pontife sur le mariage des infidèles" in *Revue de Droit Canonique*, 10–11 (1960–61), pp. 98–99.

[25] P. García Barriuso, "Disolución posible de matrimonios meramente legítimos ante el derecho canónico" in *Revista española de Derecho canónico*, 16 (1961), p. 471.

chosen to reply in the Council hall with a few of the common-
places of the official theology, a reply later expanded in a maga-
zine article.[26] Some newsmen were more sympathetic to Archbishop Zoghby's initiative and they published his views, though
without too much conviction.

In 1967 Pospishil's *Divorce and Remarriage* appeared. A historical and sociological study, it concludes that the Church has
the power, for certain reasons to be formulated by the ecclesiastical authorities themselves, to dissolve a marriage both ratified
and consummated.[27] His initiative has been followed by several
noteworthy articles in United States reviews, of which the most
striking was Rosemary Ruether's "Divorce, No Longer Unthinkable,"[28] which develops an interesting interpersonal viewpoint
regarding the fact of breach of the conjugal union.

The history of the Roman Catholic position on the dissolubility of consummated sacramental marriage already suggests an
ambivalence which will become more pronounced through reflection on the data. The negative attitude of the present discipline
is in fact far more monolithic than the arguments on which the
discipline rests. The main basis for the claim of absolute indissolubility seems to be the sacramental reality of the marriage.
The examination of this issue when discussing the sacramental
bond, however, led to the conclusion that the mysterious reality
which is symbolized does not cause an essential change in the
reality of the marriage. In addition, the theological systematization surrounding indissolubility develops some paradoxes not
easy to resolve. In the first place, if the binding force is rooted
in the sacrament, the presence of the sacrament would immediately create an absolute indissolubility. Yet the Church dissolves non-consummated sacramental marriages, and this leads
to a number of efforts to explain which all add up to an extremely
complicated picture of the sacrament of matrimony.

Another viewpoint not easy to accept is that the indissolu-

[26] Charles Journet, "Le mariage indissoluble" in *Nova et Vetera*, 1966,
No. 1. Reprinted in *La Documentation Catholique*, 63 (1966), col. 1075ff.
[27] For Pospishil's book, see the Bibliography.
[28] *Commonweal*, April 14, 1967, p. 117.

bility rests on the act of consummation. It is far from clear what element in the conjugal act demands the inseparability of those who perform it. Besides, the fact of consummation is so hard to prove that Rome's own jurists would not take it as the criterion, preferring the fact of life in common freely accepted. From the strictly legal point of view, it is not very sensible to rest a strict legal prescription on such slippery ground, so that even many Catholic jurists are quite unhappy about it.[29]

A further aspect is even harder to understand. The indissolubility of marriage is a teaching that involves very serious presuppositions and consequences, and it should accordingly be presented with the greatest coherence. Recent theology, however, has tried to avoid this need by asserting in a loud voice that indissolubility is a natural concomitant of marriage. Even natural marriages are indissoluble. And still the Church dissolves them. The one society on earth to defend the indissolubility of marriage also claims to be the only one that can lawfully dissolve it.

The reason offered for this paradox is the good of the faith. But it is not clear how one can justify favoring the supernatural order by changing the natural order (to use the conventional terms). On the contrary, it would be reasonable to expect the Roman Church to defend indissolubility to the limit in all cases. The stated explanation is that this would be a type of intransigence contrary to the spirit of the gospel, because there are painful cases in which the Church can help by allowing the dissolution of a bond that has ceased to be bearable.

Such an explanation calls for another question. What strange concern is this which provides for "outsiders" (1 Cor 5:12) while forgetting "those inside the church"? What is the curious condescension that can be applied to the unbelievers while forbidden to those who "are no longer under the law" (Rom 6:14)? "For you were called to freedom" (Gal 5:13), but in certain

---

[29] Proof of the fact of consummation in the marriage courts lends itself to endless deceptions and abuses. The chapters devoted to this theme in the manuals of canon law procedure constitute in themselves a complete condemnation of the system that requires them. Today's Christian accepts an incarnate Church, but not to the point where certain religious decisions call systematically for the inspection of the woman's private parts.

respects canon law acknowledges greater freedom to those not yet incorporated into Christ.

The conclusion to be drawn from these reflections is that the Church cannot continue to sustain the indissolubility of marriage by reason of its validity and consummation. However, it does not follow that the Church should now set up procedures for dissolving such marriages. The starting point should rather be the complete rejection of the legal and social structures for marriage in the Church. The Church does not join and separate. It does not regulate the unions and the disunions of men. There is no ecclesiastical criterion to determine the social validity of a marriage, and in consequence none to determine its invalidity. The function of the Church is simply to urge its own norms regarding marriage on the community of the faithful. The observance of these norms merely determines the religious value of the marriage, and can also be a condition for membership of the community.

In consequence, the Church should limit itself to promoting, by means consonant with Christian principles, the absolute and perpetual faithfulness of spouses, excluding in appropriate cases from the community of the faithful those who transgress. That, in strictly evangelical language, is what it means to say that Christian marriage is indissoluble.

II. An Essay in Historical Synthesis

The history of marriage in Catholic dogma must go beyond noting progress and approving each of its elements. It should also set out the internal laws of this evolution and establish what are the deep tensions which give meaning to and explain the results historically established. The first part of this chapter showed how slight is the cohesion of the Catholic doctrinal system regarding marriage, with an analysis of five of its basic formulations. It is now appropriate to determine how this situation developed.

A first glance suggests that Catholic marriage theory has been marked by the two great historical facts of the establishment of medieval Christianity and the Protestant Reformation. Deeper study, however, shows that these explanations are insufficient.

They fail to take account of the internal dynamism of the religious, social and ethical ideas themselves which were held concerning marriage, a human fact of the first order. A series of tensions developed between the religious, juridic, individual and social aspects of marriage on the one hand, and the various moral, philosophical, theological and political ideologies of society on the other. The dynamism of these tensions was what basically determined the evolution of the ideas, although of course the great shocks which marked the history of Christianity also contributed.

The contrasting paths taken by the East and West from a single starting point make it easier to study the evolution of marriage. Whereas the developments of the two Churches are complementary in other dogmatic areas, here they are in contrast. The reason for the divergence is important.

1. *Religious evaluation and moral evaluation*

The first tension to arise was between the religious evaluation of marriage and its moral evaluation. Christian canonical writings have a view of marriage as a holy reality instituted by God (Gen 2:18–24; 1:26–28). Jesus said that the action of God is present in every human union: "What therefore God has joined together, let no man put asunder" (Mt 19:6). But the point that brings out most clearly the sacred meaning of marriage is its ability to convert itself into an expressive symbol of religious realities. In the Old Testament, the marriage union is taken to represent the alliance of God with his people. The prophet Hosea was the first to use this image, followed by Jeremiah, Isaiah, and Ezekiel.[30] The Song of Solomon derives its imagery entirely from nuptial poetry. St. Paul carries the symbol into the Christian mystery. For him, the intimate union of husband and wife is a figurative sign of the union of Christ and the Church (Eph 5:22–32).

Later Christian reflection concentrated on determining more precisely the scope and meaning of this symbolism. The scripture statements seem clear enough in themselves, especially the

[30] Hos 1–3; Jer 2:2; 3:1–13; Is 54:4–8; 62:3–5; Ezek 16–23.

concept of "the two in one flesh" as the symbol of the intimate union of Christ and the Church.[31] The Greek Fathers take the statement as it is and exalt the union of husband and wife by investing it with religious meaning and proclaiming it a source of grace. They are not afraid to speak of the love of the spouses,[32] although retaining their reservations regarding sexual relations.[33]

Latin writers, on the contrary, offer a silent but unified resistance to accepting the symbolism in all its fullness. Their notion of the union of man and wife is deficient and negative,[34] and the union in consequence lacks in their eyes sufficient value to symbolize by itself the mystery of Christ and the Church.

This attitude is most obvious in Augustine. Although he admitted in his early writings that the wife was the spiritual helper of her husband,[35] he later adopted the view of Ambrose that the wife is her husband's helper only to the extent to which she serves him for procreation.[36] One who started from that position could not possibly understand how the union of husband

[31] Methodius of Olympus (3rd century) describes this intimate relationship of Christ and the Church in specifically nuptial terms: "The Word left his heavenly Father and came down on earth in order to cling to his spouse, and slept in the ecstasy of His Passion, . . . and like a woman the Church conceives of this seed" (*Symposium*, III, 8, A.C.W., 27, 65).

[32] "When the man and the woman join in marriage, they no longer appear as something of this earth, but as the image of God himself" (St. John Chrysostom, *Homilia 26 in 1 Cor*). "Marriage is the mystery of love" (St. John Chrysostom, *Homilia in 1 Cor* 7, 39). "From Adam to the Lord, authentic conjugal love was the perfect sacrament" (St. Ephraem, *In Epheseos*, 5, 32). "What can be nearer to a man than his own wife, or rather, his own flesh?" (St. Basil, *Epistolae*, 160, 4. PG 32, 628). All these texts are quoted by Eudokimov, *Le Mariage*, pp. 75ff.

[33] Origen distinguishes love from love. "Husbands, love your wives, says the Apostle. But he did not stop there. He knew that there is a certain love of husbands, even for their own wives, which is dishonorable, and another love that pleases God. And in order to show how husbands should love their wives, he made the point perfectly clear. Husbands, he says, love your wives as Christ has loved the Church" (*In Cant. hom.*, II, 1).

[34] St. Ambrose writes: "It is for the sake of the generation of the human race that woman was joined to man" (*De Paradiso*, 10. PL 14, 298).

[35] *De Gen. contra Manich.*, II, 11. PL 34, 204 (written in 389).

[36] *De Gen. ad litteram*, 9, 5. PL 34, 396. See *Contra Jul. Pelag.*, II, 7, 20. PL 44, 688.

and wife could by itself have the ability to evoke a spiritual mystery. The text of Eph 5:32 is explained as referring to Adam and Eve, and the words of Adam ("the two shall become one") are interpreted as a prophecy about Christ and the Church.[37] The marriage of Christians is reduced to secondary importance in the mystery. It represents the indissolubility of the union of Christ and the Church, and for this reason it is a "sacrament," that is to say, a sacred bond.[38]

One can see at work in the whole of this process the insidious genius of encratism which to a greater or lesser extent infected all the moral teaching of the early Christian theologians. Its impact on the notion of marriage has already been discussed.[39] Here can be seen how it prevents a fully religious view of the marriage union. The "becoming one" of the two spouses was not capable of being raised to the level of a mystery. Marriage was a lower state. Unless it was ennobled with virginal values, it closed the path to perfection. And if any part of it was entitled to be raised to the level of a mystery, this could only be the bond, the word irrevocably given. It was as though the spouses were not two in one flesh but two in one word.

For a thousand years such moral prejudices held back in the West the development of the profoundly religious values of Christian marriage. It did not matter that it was given every kind of religious ornament as regards its secondary aspects, and that praise for chaste spouses is on the lips of every Church Father. The essential reality of conjugal life continued to be regarded with suspicion and kept on the margin of spiritual growth. Nevertheless, the biblical message was too clear. Its invitation to look at the vigorous symbolism contained in the union of the spouses was too insistent. The tension rose to a critical level in the early scholastic period, but other problems and tensions intervened to alter the balance of forces, resulting in victory for the view of Augustine.

[37] *De Gen. ad litteram,* 9, 19. PL 34, 408; *De nupt. et concup.,* II, 32, 54. PL 44, 468.
[38] *De nupt. et concup.,* I, 10, 11. PL 44, 420.
[39] pp. 89ff, above.

2. *The juridic and the human-religious views*

The second area of tension was between the juridic view of marriage and the human-religious view. As the Roman Empire weakened and decayed, the life of the Church was deeply affected by the changes occurring in the political and social context of the West. The civil authorities were weak and dispersed. They found themselves often unable to conduct public affairs properly. The Church had to take over social institutions of primary importance, like education and marriage, in order to ensure their continuity. This assumption of competence did not result from a conscious decision. It was a gradual process, and it went hand in hand with the growing influence of the city bishops over the *comes*, the official guardian of the social order who was also an heir to Rome's municipal traditions. The ecclesiastical and civil courts often worked together, until in the end matrimonial and many other issues came under the exclusive competence of the former.

But if the actual assertion of competence was gradual and spontaneous, the justification was a conscious act involving a stand with the gravest consequences. The restoration of the Empire of the West carried with it the idea of a kingdom of Christians, that is to say, of a political entity all of whose subjects would profess Christianity. The word *Christendom* employed in this sense first made its appearance in the ninth century,[40] but the idea was developed by Pope John VIII (872–882), who defined the Roman Church as "the one with authority over all peoples, the one in which the nations of the whole world are united as their only mother and only head."[41] The ideas of these 9th-century popes took clear shape in the 11th century with Gregory VII and his following of theorizers known as the "Gregorians." The result was the establishment in Europe of a theocracy which brought together ideas from Leo the Great, Augustine, and Ambrose and vested itself in the tradition

---

40 In a letter of Pope Nicholas I (858–867) to Emperor Michael.
41 Quoted by Etienne Gilson, *History of Christian Philosophy in the Middle Ages* (New York, Random House, 1955).

of the four Books of Kings of the Old Testament and the supremacy of the priests over the people of Israel.

Against this background, the marriage problems which preoccupied the theologians of the 11th and 12th centuries can be seen more clearly. They sought to create a legal structure to respond to the sacred and Christian concept of marriage, while simultaneously adapted to the needs of civil and public order. The Christian theorizers had to contend with enormous difficulties. A theoretic system of marriage in its religious reality did not exist, and the concepts of Roman law reflected in great part a social situation long since disappeared. The new conditions required their own law, and an important one of them was the social and economic change resulting from the decline of feudalism and the flourishing of the free cities. Protection of the children and of the wife called for social arrangements in which the law would assume the protective role formerly played by the clan or extended family. And all of this, it must be remembered, had to be done by appeal to Christian principles and without a violent break with tradition.

The most urgent problem was to determine whether the essence of marriage lay in the contract or the consummation. National and family customs complicated the issue by distinguishing betrothal, which already created some obligations, and the marriage contract. Roman law had the same distinction, but the Christian practice had ignored the betrothal and tended to stress the marriage blessing. To avoid confusion between the betrothal promise and the contract, a thesis came into favor which placed the essence of marriage in cohabitation understood as the actual physical union of the spouses. The suggestion was found already in Hincmar of Reims in the 9th century,[42] and was taken up by Gratian and the Bologna school.[43] The development of the dispute between them and the French theologians who held that the essence was the contract has been noted

---

[42] *Epistolae*, 22. PL 126, 151–152.
[43] Hincmar and Gratian, though three centuries apart, agreed as followers of Isidore of Seville. Isidore's concept of sacrament, much closer to the Greeks than to Augustine, may have contributed to the restressing of the mysterious content of the "being one sole flesh" of the spouses.

already.[44] The different trends within the dynamism of the basic ideological tensions will now be sketched.

The French view was based on the Latin tradition and St. Augustine. The Christian jurists had interpreted in their own way the aphorism of Roman law formulated by Ulpianus as: *"Nuptias consensus non concubitus facit"* (Consent and not co-habitation makes a marriage). They understood consent to mean the act of consenting and concluded that as soon as that act was performed, the marriage was a completed fact. In this inter-pretation they were mistaken, because the Roman jurists had understood consent not as the act of consenting but the fact of living together freely and publicly. The position of Augustine and the Paris school thus constituted a further step in the isola-tion and downgrading of the specific values of married life, a process already observed as characteristic of Latin theology. It finds the essence of marriage in an element which is largely independent of the characteristic constituents of married life, an element defined legally—a contract. All "the rest" is secondary.[45]

The thesis that placed the essence of marriage in specifically conjugal elements had, however, an important argument on its side. Custom, confirmed by various synods, authorized the dis-solution of a non-consummated marriage if one of the spouses entered religious life. This meant that a marriage only "ratified" (the contract) was still imperfect, and that the full quality of marriage came only with consummation. The Italian school relied on this concrete fact more than on theological reflection on the mystery of Christ and the Church as signified by the conjugal union.[46] The popes of the 11th and 12th centuries, while agreeing with the Paris school, recognized at the same time the possibility of dissolving the bond before consummation, resolving the problem but intensifying the difficulty. There the issue still rests.

[44] pp. 139f. See also pp. 130f.

[45] So stated by Pope Nicholas I in his *Letter to the Bulgarians* (PL 119, 9800). See also Denzinger 334.

[46] The theme was recalled by Hincmar (*loc. cit.*) and taken up again in the 12th century by Hugo of St. Victor in *De Beatae Mariae Virginitate*, 4 (PL 176, 874). See *D. T. C.*, IX, cols. 2144–2147. But it withered in the unfavorable climate of the Middle Ages.

The need existed to determine not only the exact juridic situation but also the sacramental value of marriage. Agreeing that marriage is the contract itself, what is the essence of the sacrament? Is it the contract or something added to the contract? The question became important from the 11th century onwards, when the errors of Berengarius of Tours concerning the Eucharist, backed by a remarkable analysis of St. Augustine's writings, forced the theologians to clarify the notion of sacrament, and to base their views also on those of Augustine. They came up with the definition of a sacrament as "the visible sign of an invisible reality." In marriage, the sign could be sought in one of two elements, the contract or the consummation. As might be anticipated, the sacrament was identified with the contract.

There were two reasons for this decision. First, the most widely held view placed the essence of marriage itself in the contract, not the consummation, with the almost inescapable deduction that the sacrament must be rooted where the marriage was. Second, the Augustinian theory gave a religious value to marriage exclusively on the ground of the indissolubility of the consent that was given, and that consent was described as a "sacramentum." It was that bond and nothing else that—in this view—recalled the mystery of the union of Christ and his Church.

The poverty of the vision of Augustine was thus clearly placed on the record. By applying to marriage the conceptual components of the recently established category of sacrament, the medieval theologians changed the legal element in marriage into the sign, leaving outside the significant or sacramental area all the other aspects of the complex human reality. The faithful Christian was invited to consider his fidelity to the word given in marriage as a symbol of the perpetuity of the union of Christ and his Church. But the spouses were not invited to see their committed and total love as a sign of any higher mystery.[47] The Middle Ages had no married theologians. The teaching on marriage was developed by celibates. They sought their data in the writings of celibate Fathers, and their conclusions were copied by celibate monks and formulated in disciplinary canons by

[47] And if occasionally they were invited to do so, it is because the Spirit breathes where he will, overcoming even theological rigor.

celibate bishops and abbots. Only the wandering troubadours felt the need to sing the praises of a love which nobody was willing to sanctify for them.

By the 12th century marriage was definitely established as one of the Seven Sacraments. It had, nevertheless, entered by the service door. The theologians, and in particular the most influential theologian of the period, Peter Lombard, denied that it conferred grace. Marriage was merely "a remedy for concupiscence."[48] St. Thomas in the 13th century had progressed to the point where he thought it "more probable" that marriage conferred grace,[49] but the canonists up to the 14th century continued to doubt.

A system so inadequate and so indifferent to the human and even the religious values of marriage could only deteriorate under the weight of its own incoherence. A sacrament is a basic spiritual reality in Christianity. Alongside or in connection with the Scriptures, it is the privileged place for God's revelation to every man. The scholastics defined a sacrament as the outstanding sign of the mysteries of Christ. But marriage, in the state to which the legal-minded theologians had reduced it, provided very few points of support for a spiritual meaning. The result was the formulation of a theory that the sacramental reality came to it from some extrinsic addition. Duns Scotus took the final step in the 14th century by applying the hylomorphic theory to the sacrament of matrimony. Christ, he said, when raising the natural contract to the dignity of a sacrament, had to add something to it, at least the words constituting the form of the sacrament. In consequence, the contract is merely the matter of the sacrament and not the sacrament itself.[50]

The influence of Scotus was considerable[51] and it helped to spread the idea that a valid non-sacramental marriage of Christians was possible. Melchior Cano in particular adopted this view

---

48 Peter Lombard, *Sententiae*, IV, dist. 26, c. 1–4 and 6. Peter Lombard here follows Abelard, the one who started to develop theology as a science. He said that since marriage does not produce grace, it is not a sacrament like the others (*Epitome Theologiae Christianae*, c. 31. PL 178, 1745).
49 *In IV Sententiae*, dist. 26, q. 2, a. 3. (See *Suppl.*, q. 42, a. 3).
50 Duns Scotus, *Op. Oxon.*, *In IV Sent.*, dist. 26, q. 1, n. 14.
51 See Le Bras in *D. T. C.*, IX, col. 2204.

in the 16th century, under the extreme form that the priest is the minister of the sacrament of matrimony. Without following the vicissitudes of this theory further, it is appropriate to note that it originated in purely doctrinal speculations and was not influenced by political considerations. It is true that the separation of the contract (as a purely civil aspect of marriage) and the sacrament did give rise to jurisdictional conflicts between the Church and the civil courts of some states from the 12th century onwards.[52] The lay jurists, however, based their stand not on the Scotist teaching but on a general theory of church-state relations different from that of the popes of Christendom.[53] Occasionally, especially in the Gallican period, jurists appealed to the Scotist distinction to justify the claims of the state, but in the Middle Ages the issue raged exclusively on the theological level.

The point is not without importance. It places the Scotist thesis and related theories in the uninterrupted line of the negative and pessimist attitudes toward the intrinsic values of natural marriage. This position, as should by now be clear, must be kept in mind as a key to the evolution of theological teaching on marriage ever since the time of St. Augustine.

To sum up, scholasticism established three points of Catholic teaching on marriage. It is a sacrament. The sacrament is the contract itself. It is indissoluble by reason of its sacramental quality. The attention of the theologians centered on the juridic element, making it the specific point of location of the sacramental element. The human value and spiritual meaning of the conjugal community were overlooked, and the call of St. Paul in his letter to the Ephesians[54] did not prove strong enough to draw attention to them. The fact is that married life is not considered in a personal perspective in the thought of the Middle Ages. Marriage is an institution at the service of the species, not

---

[52] *Ibid.*, col. 2220–2221.

[53] Marsilius of Padua (14th century) was the principal representative of the new theory. William of Occam backed him theologically. See Le Bras, *loc. cit.*

[54] Eph 5:32. See, for example, the superficial commentary of St. Thomas Aquinas in *In IV Sent.*, dist. 26, q. 2, a. 1, and the somewhat better treatment in *Suppl.*, q. 42, a. 1.

of the individual. It is admitted that in the actual condition of fallen mankind marriage can also serve as a remedy for concupiscence, for the lust which drives one sex toward the other.[55] The love of the spouses is not a factor,[56] except in so far as it can be inserted into higher categories of love, of which the model is friendship or "love of benevolence."[57] The spouses unite "in a single flesh" to produce offspring. Every conjugal act performed without this purpose is at least a backsliding from the Christian ideal of marriage, if not a sin.[58]

Domestic life itself is regarded with indifference by the first scholastics, and when they refer to the wife, some do not hesitate to join the anti-feminist chorus of popular literature.[59] One can always find, not far under the surface, the influence of the diatribe against marriage in St. Jerome's *Adversus Jovinianum*.[60]

Faced with the lamentable procession of men and women to the altar, the theologians struggled to locate the sacrament, the holy thing, as far as possible away from the stagnant pond of concupiscence. To do this, they had first of all to drain the scripture texts about marriage of their exalted and extremely human religious impulse. Here, the advance work of Augustine was of great help. It enabled them to set up the contract as a fortress and to store there all the discoveries of theological speculation about the sacraments. From St. Thomas onwards, they had also the backing of Aristotle, who reminded them that marriage is a natural institution at the service of the species.

Indissolubility fitted perfectly in this picture. While estab-

---

[55] According to Peter Lombard, the purpose of procreation no longer applies, because the world is already sufficiently populated, and in consequence marriage is permitted only as a remedy for concupiscence (*Sententiae*, IV, d. 26, c. 1–4).

[56] The only two scholastics to exalt married love, and even they raised it to a mystic level approaching deincarnation, were Hugo of St. Victor (*De Beata Maria Virgine*, 1. PL 176,864), and St. Bonaventure (*In IV Sent.*, d. 26, a. 2, q. 3; d. 28, a. 1, q. 6).

[57] For example, St. Thomas Aquinas, *Contra Gentiles*, III, 123.

[58] Grave, according to Rufinus (*Summa*, causa 32, q. 2); light, according to others.

[59] Such as John of Salisbury, *Polycraticus*, 8, 11. PL 199, 148–156.

[60] See P. Delhaye, "Le Dossier anti-matrimonial de l'Adversus Jovinainum et son influence sur quelques écrits latin du XII siècle" in *Medieval Studies*, 13 (1952), pp. 65–86.

lished in the canonical discipline from the 8th century, its doctrinal justification had to wait the rebirth of Augustinianism in the 12th. Indissolubility expresses a property of the bond. If marriage consists essentially in the bond, indissolubility becomes an essential property of marriage. It was also the reason given for its sacramental quality. As Augustine had said, it was a "sacramentum" because it was a word that could not be taken back. Marriage was thus joined to the mystery, but only to one aspect of the mystery, and that determined the characteristics of its meaningful image. As Augustine had been the first to recognize, natural marriage could be dissolved. Only to the extent that it was an image of Christ and the Church was marriage indissoluble.

Indissolubility, nevertheless, allowed exceptions. Tradition and custom suggested some. The principal exceptions were adultery and the entry of one of the spouses into religion. The medieval jurists rejected the former but retained the latter. The ground of dissolution for adultery had the support of a reasonable interpretation of the gospel, of the practice of the East, of some Latin canons, and of motives of human consideration for innocent persons. The ground of entrance into the religious life was supported by a disciplinary tradition and by arguments carrying weight in monastic circles. The monks had influence and the laity had none. One ground was admitted and the other rejected. The facts, when put this way, seem a caricature, but they are the facts. The people who then governed society were not particularly concerned whether or not innocent spouses abandoned as a result of adultery could remarry, but the dissolution of marriage by entry into a monastery or convent solved some acute problems of the ruling classes.[61] This dissolution was granted even before it has been determined where the essence of marriage lay, and it was then understood that the marriage was simply undone. Later it was laid down that divorce in this case was possible only before consummation, although it has not

[61] The concession of dissolution for entering a religious order, because of the social context, resolved various problems characteristic of the ruling class (such as political marriages) but benefited the lower classes practically not at all.

yet been explained how a sacrament which is indissoluble precisely by reason of its being a sacrament can be dissolved. The efforts of the medieval thinkers had accordingly produced the following result. The legal aspect of marriage prevailed over its existential aspect. The individual found himself subjected to and bound by the double law of the institution and of the mystery, as partially applied. Morality fought with religion, law with life. But the current of spiritual life which God had introduced into the midst of the conjugal community still flowed underground, until it burst out in the decisive tension which placed and continues to place man in opposition to things.

3. *The juridico-religious view and individual rights*

The third tension arose between the legal and religious view of marriage on one side, and the rights of the individual on the other. The ideological renewal which characterized the beginning of what we call the modern era in regard to all aspects of human life had only a slight influence—and even that quite late—on the Catholic understanding of marriage. Two related facts contributed to this relative stagnation, the Protestant Reformation and the Council of Trent.

From the 15th century, theology was influenced anew by ancient Greece and Rome. The classics then rediscovered included the Hebrew and Greek scriptures and the Eastern Fathers in their original languages. Biblical and patristic exegesis clarified many ideas and gave rise to new problems. Meanwhile, profane thought exercised pressure on theology by proclaiming the pre-eminence of individual values, especially freedom. The individual began to emancipate himself from the ideological and institutional tutelage of the regime of Christendom, while a new theory of the state was being worked out and was in places being put in practice without waiting for a complete formulation of the theory.

The teaching of the Middle Ages on marriage was bound to be criticized from many points of view. Its religious dimension had been fully explained. The characteristic of absolute indissolubility ran into serious contradictions in the patristic tradition.

The exclusive jurisdiction of the Church was justifiable only by the still shaky theory of identity of contract and sacrament. Finally, the narrow legal Latin molds were unsuited to the situations found in the mission lands of the recently discovered new world.

The complete break of the Protestant Reformation included the abandonment of the medieval position on marriage. The Reformers professed a high esteem for the married state,[62] but they did not regard it as a sacrament. They saw it instead as a purely natural institution,[63] and as such fully under the jurisdiction of the secular power. Divorce was authorized in various cases, with the Scripture rules providing the guidelines.

Catholic reaction was limited to reaffirming the aspects of the medieval arrangement rejected by the Reformation, thereby blocking the possibility of a progressive and peaceful evolution of the teaching. Catholic discipline on marriage drew progressively further away from the needs of the new society, and the disputes with the opponents served merely to establish more intransigent positions. The crisis became evident first in the field of public law.

The Middle Ages had set up a legal system, the subjects of which were considered to be Christians living within the regime of Christendom. The new Europe, on the contrary, was composed of individuals belonging to a state. It did not take long for tension to build up in the area of marriage law. The Church had assumed complete control over marriage, so that the states found themselves without any institutions or facilities for dealing with this aspect of society. The reaction came first in France with Gallicanism in the 17th century, and then in Austria with Josephism in the 18th.

The first issue was the possibility of a valid and lawful marriage falling entirely under the jurisdiction of the state. There

---

[62] "God has blessed this state above all others" (Luther, *Catechismus Maior*, I, VI Praec. Decal.). "The most sacred bond that God has placed between us is that which unites husband and wife" (Calvin, Sermon 41 on the Ephesians, in *Corpus Reformatorum*, 79, col. 761).

[63] "Ein weltlich eusserlich Ding" (Luther, *Werke*, vol. 32, 377).

was no desire in principle to deny the religious value of marriage, but to affirm a parallel civil value. The question could be formulated in several ways. The most moderate view accepted a double power over marriage, civil and religious, corresponding to its double entity, arguing that the sacrament did not change the contractual nature of a marriage.[64] The most extreme took its stand on the difference between the contract and the sacrament recognized by some theologians from the 14th century,[65] and denied the Church all power over the contract.[66]

The appearance of civil marriage with the consequent admission of divorce brought into the open the true directions of the struggle being waged between the Church of Rome and the states of Europe. What the Church tried to do in the 19th century was to defend the legal statute of a social and political situation which had long since disappeared, the statute of Christendom. For more than three centuries, ever since the Protestant Reformation, the Catholic Church had refused to recognize the fact that the countries of Europe were no longer inhabited exclusively by Christians giving allegiance to the Roman see. For that reason, in the same way as it would not recognize the validity of marriages entered into by Protestants (claiming a defect of form),[67] it continued for a longer time to refuse to recognize that there were in the society individuals who were not Christians (although baptized) and therefore admitted no valid marriage for them. Every non-canonical marriage between two baptized persons, even if they had openly abandoned the Christian faith, was judged a mere concubinage.[68]

The conflict over jurisdiction concealed a sharper and deeper one, the assertion of the rights of the individual vis-à-vis the

---

[64] Gerbais defended this view in *Traité pacifique des empêchements du mariage*, 1690.

[65] See p. 102, above.

[66] This is the thesis presented by Launoy in *Tractatus de iure saecularium principum christianorum in sanciendis impedimentis matrimonium dirimentibus*, 1674.

[67] This situation was not fully clarified until Pius X's *Ne temere* decree, issued in August 1907 and in effect from April 19, 1908. See p. 126, above.

[68] Pius IX expressed himself in this precise sense in a protest against the institution of civil marriage in the Republic of New Granada (Colombia) in 1852.

institution.[69] The Catholic theory of marriage subjected individual rights to a tight control based on a very special understanding of the notions of "contract" and "institution." Three aspects of the system, in particular, ran counter to the mentality of modern man. First there was the anthropological poverty of the definition of marriage as a contract. Next, there was the absolute subordination under all circumstances of the person to the institution, of the individual to the species; and this tension was further aggravated by the fact that the most rigid property of marriage as conceived by Catholic theology, its indissolubility, derived from purely religious demands. Finally, there was the aggressively all-embracing attitude of the Church. Its laws sought to compel every baptized person to submit to religious demands, leaving no place for a non-religious use of his right to marry.

The claim that the contract and the sacrament are distinct, and the series of political clashes over jurisdiction are merely manifestations of the general freedoms. The first democratic or liberal political regimes set up in society a neutral space, nonconfessional and removed from religious totalitarianism. In this space the citizen who was not a Christian or who left the Christian community into which he had been baptized could shake off the previously imposed religious trappings and move in full freedom. Such an attitude was in fact in total agreement with the teaching of the New Testament on the free acceptance of the faith, but the Church of Rome was unwilling to recognize its social and institutional consequences. For that reason, the tension affecting marriage in modern times was between the individual finally conscious of his rights and a rigidly legal and religious conception of marriage, which unduly restricted those rights.

The romantic and liberal individualism of the 18th century, however, was destined to exercise a very limited influence on a Catholic society mobilized for defense. The tension had its effect on the dealings of the Church with the outside, without affecting for the time being its internal institutions. A lay world was born

---

[69] Rights sometimes expressed very ingenuously: "The ability to divorce flows from individual freedom, which would be lost by an indissoluble commitment" (Laws of the French Republic, law of September 20, 1792).

and grew to one side of and parallel with the world of religion, each remaining closed to the other. Finally, however, the individualistic ferment deep in middle-class society burst out from its political and social conditionings. The result was a new formulation in which Christian thought could finally recognize its contribution, the personalist view of marriage.

4. *The personalist resolution of the tensions*

In a simplified form, yet without violence to the objective facts, the Catholic theory of marriage has been presented as the fruit of a long and far from peaceful development. A major role was played by three tensions or oppositions which were characterized by different and conflicting moral, religious, legal and social conceptions of marriage. The teaching finally fixed by Roman orthodoxy was not the result of the spontaneous impact of all these forces, but the affirmation on dogmatic grounds of one aspect of the warring concepts. The result is that the internal tensions remain hidden within the present official Catholic system.

The key to the modern view of marriage is its insertion in a context of interpersonal relations. The human and moral value of marriage is rooted in the community of persons. This view overcomes and renders inoperative all the moral reservations accumulated through the centuries by Christian theological speculation as regards the components of the marriage community.

It is precisely in the strictly religious area that the personalist approach is most effective in relieving tensions. The interpersonal community, the total self-giving, the fusion of lives, all these are converted into the very reality that signifies the divine mysteries and constitutes the specific element on which the sacramental character of marriage can rest. The other aspects, the legal and social ones, drop to second place and lose all religious relevance. The perfect union, of which the bodily union in one flesh is the realization and symbol, is freed of all pseudo-moral and pesudospiritual suspicions and is restored to its right place as the fundamental kernel of the theology of marriage. In this perspective, such issues as the identity of contract and sacrament, or the sacramental properties of the legal marriage bond, no longer have meaning. The legal components of marriage are now discarded sacramentals. Their sacred quality comes from their participation in the source of religious value constituted by the community of life of the spouses. The indissolubility of the bond, in particular, falls entirely outside any religious perspective. It is subject only to human and natural considerations.

The personalist view thus overcomes the two tensions described as the tension between the moral and the religious evaluations of marriage, and that between the juridic and the human-religious views of marriage. The religious evaluation of marriage is no longer limited by reservations concerning the moral value of the acts which constitute it, and this renewed religious concept acquires absolute primacy over the legal constructs which had tried to restrict it.

The last of the tensions is also resolved by the personalist view of the marriage union. Marriage can be seen as an institution, but it is—like all social institutions—at the service of the person. To think of a man merely as an individual can lead to subordinating him to institutional interests. Individuality is a quantitative concept, while the notion of person is qualitative and remains unaltered throughout all types of social groupings. The man and woman who marry do not dissolve their personalities in the neutral element of the institution.

The consequence is that the institution is not entitled to impose conditions that would limit the fundamental rights of the person. Neither can the religious attributes of the institution suppress such rights. It is quite clear, accordingly, that the basic right to religious freedom rooted in the dignity of the human person remains even when a baptized person enters the institution of marriage. To adopt the married state and to receive a sacrament are two distinct decisions, and they pertain to different social and spiritual spheres. Every man, even if baptized, remains free, when exercising his right to the marriage union, either to receive a sacrament or not to receive it. The sacraments are offered, not imposed. In consequence, marriage can be validly and lawfully contracted without conferring at the same time a sacrament.

Another of the consequences of the primacy of the person over the institution concerns the indissolubility of the bond.[70] Society cannot weigh down an institution with properties that restrict the fundamental rights of the person. One such right is to form a family, and absolute indissolubility is an impediment to the exercise of this right in some situations, especially in the case of abandonment.[71] In addition, as we have already shown, no substantial religious reasons for indissolubility exist. Respect for the fundamental rights of the human person demands, therefore, that the social institution of marriage recognize a certain number of causes for separation and remarriage, the particular causes to be determined according to changing circumstances.

This brief survey suffices to show that the old controversies about marriage retain little importance today, because the serious tensions which underlay them have been resolved. The elements which effected their resolution have long ago become an integral part of the mentality of contemporary mankind. What remains is for the ecclesiastical decision makers to get a clear understanding of the consequences of having accepted the personalist assumptions of the man of our time, and to adapt the disciplinary structures to a set of concepts that can be taken as definitely established even in the theological area.

5. *The dialectic continues*

This chapter opened by noting the fact that a crisis currently affects the Catholic theory of marriage. It then examined successively the broad outlines of the situation from two viewpoints, the static (analyzing five basic formulations of the system), and the dynamic (studying the historical and ideological process which led to these formulations). That in turn led to the conclusion that Catholic teaching on marriage lacks internal co-

---

[70] An Orthodox writer points out this correlation very clearly: "The principle of dissolution depends on the primacy of the common good over the particular case, of the general over the personal. But from the divine viewpoint, the gospel says that the soul is unique and is more precious than the world and the common good. These are values that cannot be compared with each other" (P. Eudokimov, *op. cit.*, p. 117).

[71] The limitations which result from the common good were discussed on pp. 160f.

herence and does not fit properly into the theological edifice of Western Christianity. Examination of the historical process provided the fundamental lines of an explanation. Catholic marriage theory was developed on the margin of the deep and organic current of evolution of dogma. The determining factors were not religious realities or motivations, but rather moral, legal and political concepts and attitudes which had little or no relationship with Christianity. They included a low estimation of the married state, the formation of a theocratic Christendom, and coercion of the individual.

The final resolution of these conflicts followed the completion of the process which led from individualism to a recognition of the qualitative position of the person as explanation and ultimate criterion. Once incorporated into this current of thought, marriage appears again to the believer as the bearer of a group of human values which give it a privileged position as a source and manifestation of divine grace. Religion can see in the community of life of the spouses a sign of the saving mysteries of God. Religion will give up its attempt to change the natural reality of marriage and to control its social aspects, thereby giving a clear testimony of its respect for all that is human.

Within this explanatory framework, indissolubility can be seen in its true meaning. The doctrine of indissolubility emerges as a step in the long struggle of Christian thought and effort against the corruption of pagan marriage. What began as a negative expression (divorce as conceived by the pagans is inadmissible) was turned into a positive teaching (marriage is indissoluble because it is a sacrament) and raised to the status of an absolute principle. This attitude does not follow from the internal demands of the teaching but was added from outside and became established thanks to the rise of a particular political situation, Christendom, which allowed the Church to impose its religious discipline on the whole of society.

In this context, it can be said that the present renewal of the teaching on divorce represents a return to an earlier historical situation, but at a higher level. The renewing position cannot be described as a simple affirmation of divorce, something that would bring us back to the situation under the Roman Empire.

The new position can be understood only by starting from the position which it replaces. The thesis now presented in favor of divorce is not an absolute affirmation, but rather a reply to the particular attitude which rejects absolutely any dissolution of the bond. What is rejected is this absolute position. The valid elements in the positions being replaced are retained, and in particular their rejection of the pagan discipline on divorce. But it is not an out-and-out rejection calculated to swing the pendulum too far. The rejection of the pagan exaggerations is nuanced by a simultaneous rejection of the medieval exaggerations in the other direction. That is why it can be said that the position of the early Christians in their struggle for the integrity of marriage against pagan abuses is being repeated but at a higher level, a level which has already overcome the danger of a total exclusion of divorce.

This view of marriage and its breakdown is thus not absolute or static, but dialectic. It is dialectic first of all because it is the result of a process of analysis and division conducted by "the enormous power of the Negative."[72] It is dialectic also because it depends on the continuous interplay of such concepts as person and institution, grace and nature, individual and society. Whether in its purely social organization, its religious dimension, or the attitude of the Christian community toward the civil forms of union and breach, marriage appears as the result of a set of forces and tensions that vary according to historical circumstance. What remains is to seize and read the signs of the times.

---

[72] "Die ungeheure Macht des Negativen" (Hegel, *System der Wissenschaft*, Vorrede, Meiner ed., p. 29).

CHAPTER 6

The Way Out of the Dilemma

The problem of the innocent abandoned spouse constitutes a very specific human situation, but one that—from the legal and dogmatic viewpoints—is part of the wider issue of divorce and remarriage. For that reason, this special theme does not have its own history or doctrinal treatment. It is always inserted into broader and more general discussions. This book reflects that state of affairs. Catholic teaching on marriage and divorce had to be studied and examined as a whole in order to assemble the elements of reflection needed to develop a theory regarding the right of the innocent abandoned spouse to remarry.

Such study established that the case of the innocent abandoned spouse was given special consideration in certain historical and theological situations. The Greek Fathers, for example, accepted without discussion the right of the innocent spouse to remarry, although limiting the use of this right to the husband because of cultural assumptions. In the uneven development of marriage discipline, this issue can be said to enjoy a place of privilege, and even the intransigent canonists of the Catholic Church today prefer to overlook it when trying to justify their impositions.

Examination of the scripture texts referring to divorce has shown the need for great caution in treating the theme from the doctrinal aspect. Many exegetical questions about the principal texts still remain unanswered. The major conclusion is that neither the gospels nor St. Paul's epistles approach it from a legal standpoint. In other words, they are not thinking of the validity or invalidity of the dissolution of one marriage and the entry into another, but of the adjustment of such situations to the standards of the Christian community. These standards called for absolute fidelity of the spouses, yet admitted divorce and remarriage in certain extreme situations. Nevertheless, it would seem that the religious value of marriage was reserved for that marriage which expressed sufficiently the divine archetype, namely, a marriage that was absolutely one. The references are not sufficient to clarify this point fully. The evidence does not justify the denial of all Christian religious value to a second marriage considered lawful by the community.

The Greek patristic tradition and the Latin patristic tradition of the first centuries agree that marriage can be dissolved for the adultery of the wife, while proclaiming criteria of legal inequality of the sexes and a doctrine of spiritual perfection that makes it impossible to accept their reasoning completely as a basis for a theory favoring remarriage of the innocent spouse. The exception which the Greek and the early Latin Fathers recognize does, however, invalidate any claim that marriage is absolutely indissoluble.

Just as the doctrinal basis for the Greek position cannot be accepted in its entirety, so the intransigent attitude of the post-Constantine Latin Fathers must be rejected, because it rests on unacceptable principles. What the testimony of antiquity gives us is a valid fact, namely, that the innocent spouse could divorce and remarry. What it does not offer in general is a sufficient doctrinal explanation of that fact.

Postpatristic theological speculation concentrated on the objecive, institutional, and juridic aspects of marriage, building a complete disciplinary system on this very onesided view. The principal components of marriage, the life in common and the reciprocity of life, were completely overlooked. In consequence, it was easy to reduce to an absolute legal enactment what was merely a moral law of marriage, its need for stability.

The special situation of the innocent abandoned spouse was overlooked, because it did not constitute a legal category to be taken into account. The study in the last chapter of the evolution of teaching on marriage since the Middle Ages showed that the Catholic doctrinal system on marriage, as formulated since us it has created around the marriage contract. The Christian community would then recognize as valid all marriages performed according to the civil laws, and as equally valid divorces effected in the same way. The contractual act itself would be considered as pertaining completely to the civil order, which would mean the suppression of the canonical form of marriage. The Church would merely apply the internal standards of the Christian community, admitting to the religious life of the community those who respected those standards, and excluding all others.

These changes would automatically solve the problem of the innocent abandoned spouse. The divorce and the new marriage would call for no canonical ruling on their validity. The Christian community would simply receive the new spouses and give their union the same religious consideration as given to any marriage of the faithful.

It has, nevertheless, to be recognized that we are far from an overall solution of this kind, so that the need remains for an interim procedure to enable spouses who have done no wrong to exercise their human rights without having to abandon the religious community. The following proposal is accordingly made as one capable of being inserted into the present framework of a Church with its own legal system. The innocent abandoned spouse could, it is suggested, obtain a civil divorce and remarry civilly, with the Christian community accepting the new marriage as valid and lawful for all purposes.

The subject of this right would be the innocent party, not the guilty one. The abandonment could be at the initiative of the guilty party, or equally at that of the innocent party in cases in which the other spouse violates conjugal fidelity to the extreme of making life together impossible. The guilt or innocence would be established, not by canonical courts, but by the simple pastoral evaluation of the representatives of the Christian community and the eventual acceptance of the civil sentence. The second marriage would be civil only, or contracted before a non-Catholic clergyman with the effects of civil validity. This would mean merely that the ecclesiastical authority would not intervene legally in any way in the new marriage. The Church would pro-

the Council of Trent, cannot be accepted. It f
that the case of the innocent spouse has to be ev
regard for the implications of a doctrinal syste
historic continuity and internal coherence.

Finally, modern anthropological insights make
conception of the reality of marriage and justify
divorce and remarriage, establishing in particula
the innocent spouse. When the fact established b
exception by reason of adultery) is added to the
on the community of persons in marriage, one
to trace the lines of a general Catholic theory.
tinent to note that the Church has already acce
cally the humanism of contemporary mankind
Vatican Council's *Pastoral Constitution on the
Modern World*. The ecclesiastical decision make
drawn all the practical conclusions of this comm
needs exist, and in due course the force of t
impose itself on the rusty resistances of the past.

The only issue to be treated here is that o
abandoned spouse, but it does not necessarily f
issue is riper for decision than others. It does, ho
be more urgent and clearer. It is also an extremel
issue among social and pastoral problems, and fo
is proper to treat it apart.

I. A Proposal for Immediate Appli

The situation of the spouse abandoned in cir
which he or she is not responsible is so acute a:
emergency solution without waiting for a de
reform of the Church's attitude to marriage. Tl
tion would be to return to the simplicity of the
Christianity, when the Church neither exercised 1
right to interfere with the ordering of social and
Christian community limited itself then to lookin
affairs. The validity or invalidity of the marriages
was not regarded as falling in this category. It wa
and legal matter.

The Church of today should get rid of the en

visionally reserve to itself the right to maintain canonical marriage according to its present structure, but would allow its members to apply to the civil authorities without becoming subject to the canonical sanctions that now prevent such action.

The Christian community would regard this new marriage as on a level of equality in all respects with canonical marriage. The spouses would accordingly be admitted unconditionally to the sacraments, and the children would be recognized as legitimate for all purposes. From the Catholic viewpoint, the spouses married in this way would not be considered as in "tolerated concubinage." It is not a question of setting up a regime of pastoral tolerance for members of the faithful who have in fact gone through civil divorce and remarriage. The proposal is designed to affect the ecclesiastical legislation itself by changing it to recognize and accept this new approach. In other words, what is sought is a public declaration by the ecclesiastical authorities recognizing the social and moral validity and legality of marriage contracted in the described way.

The guilty party would, of course, not enjoy the same consideration, but would be subject to the disabilities established by the civil law, as already explained. The Christian community should adjust its judgment to the social situation accepted by the civil authorities, and therefore should not regard as concubinage a union ruled legitimate by the civil law. But it can establish the conditions for readmission to the religious life of the community of a person excluded as a guilty party.

II. Doctrinal Reasons Supporting the Proposal

1. Married life is a primary and inalienable right of every person. It is a right based on the fundamental need of union of the sexes. Marriage is thus a natural function before everything else. Raised to the category of an interpersonal relation, marriage is based on the reciprocal love of husband and wife, a love in which each finds a means to perfect and expand himself.

Marriage in its social aspect is an institution, not in the sense of owing its creation to the public authorities, but to the extent to which society develops and proposes a system of mutual relationships designed to protect and promote the use of that right.

Given the importance of marriage in the life of the community, society tends to regulate it in such a way as to benefit the group while respecting the rights of the individuals. In this perspective, limitations on the institution of marriage are legitimate, but they may not be such as to suspend systematically the exercise of the fundamental rights of the persons.

The possibility of breakdown is inherent in the interpersonal character of the marriage union of humans. The interpersonal character is based on reciprocal love, understood at least in its minimum form of harmonious cohabitation freely accepted. When such cohabitation ceases to be possible and a breach occurs, the fundamental need of married life is not thereby extinguished, and the right to it continues. Those who are separated tend to form a new family, and the social institution of marriage should facilitate their exercise of this right. It should, however, not do this indiscriminately. To oppose abuse by restraining some individual rights does not harm the common good. Social legislation should establish reasonable criteria for preventing such abuses and punishing those guilty of them. This is the reason why the social humanism of modern times seldom permits divorce by consent, a practice common in ancient societies, and recognizes only divorce pronounced by the courts. The individual whose antisocial conduct was the reason for his expulsion from the benefits of the institution will continue to exercise his rights to the community of marriage in asocial ways. But those who conform to the rules of the group cannot properly be punished in any way, and they have the right to continue their lives under the banner of the institution.

A civil marriage institution which excludes the possibility of remarriage after a breakdown of a first marriage violates the natural law, at least in the case of a person not guilty of transgressions against the community. Such an exclusion cannot be justified on religious grounds, because religion does not modify the basic moral laws. In consequence, public laws which totally restrict the rights of the person in this area must be ruled immoral, and attempts to bolster them with religious motivations are abusive. Experience confirms these assertions. Modern states which exclude divorce provide a specific type of immorality in the area of marriage, because of the multiplication of irregular situations.

2. The structure of the economy of salvation in Christ is fundamentally personal. Faith is a free human act, although lived and cultivated in community. The sacraments seek the sanctification of the Church through the sanctification of its members, and Christianity knows no example of the contrary process, namely, the irresponsible, magical and impersonal bestowal of the gifts of God on a community lacking interest in holiness.

Everything in the Church is a call to the person, and he has to answer freely. All the Church's possessions, its preaching, the sacraments, moral and disciplinary laws, are at the service of the person, beginning with the very need to be part of a community.

Christian institutions cover every aspect of human life, bringing to each situation its appropriate contribution of saving gifts. The Christian economy knows no marginal or unforeseen situations. History proves that when the ecclesiastical custom failed in some cases to adapt itself to the real needs of the people, it was custom itself that evolved until the defective institution was adjusted to provide an adequate yield. This happened, for example, with penance. "The second plank after shipwreck," the penance that could never be repeated, did not meet the needs of the masses converted to Christianity. The process was slow and not always easy to document. But the institution of penance gradually evolved into a repeatable sacrament. The very broad rules governing baptism provide another good example of the adjustment of institutions to the concrete needs of human existence. They are adapted to all foreseeable situations, and only in the most abnormal circumstances is it materially impossible to administer baptism.

Adjustment to the spiritual needs of the faithful is a requirement for Christian institutions, but the facts unfortunately show that this principle is not applied universally in the Church. While history shows some cases of notable adaptation, it shows others in which extreme maladjustment continues. In the sacramental area, for example, two rites—confirmation and anointing of the sick—are going out of style even with practicing Catholics, while no meaningful institution is available to take care of two crucial points in man's life, adolescence and grave illness.

The question here under discussion is another prime example of failure to adapt. According to established general principles, the Christian institution of marriage should help the spiritual needs of men of all times and in all situations. If there is to be any exception, it should only be that of one guilty of transgression. A man's bad conduct can make a means of salvation useless for him. What is absolutely inadmissible is that the legal structuring of the sanctifying means should prevent its efficacy in a series of foreseeable and even foreseen cases. Yet this is precisely what happens in the case of the innocent abandoned spouse. The institution in its Roman form sets up a situation in which a great number of the faithful find themselves deprived of a means morally necessary for their salvation, without any guilt on their part. It is obvious that the situation of abandonment is socially foreseeable. It receives, in fact, a legal categorization. The Catholic who finds himself without any blame in this situation is excluded by the Church's laws from the right to use a means of spiritual and human progress, one that in the final analysis is also a means of salvation, namely, marriage. Human wickedness deprived him of his first union. The imperfection of the Church prevents him from gaining a second. In this way, the Roman Catholic institution of marriage systematically drives great numbers of virtuous believers into a situation of the most bitter suffering, making them wretched by decree.

3. The biggest theological objection to the proposal just made is perhaps the sacramental character of the marriage. If the remarriage supposes the breaking of the first bond, the second marriage is a sacrament. If this is so, then the proposed change of legislation would assume that it had already been shown that the sacramental bond can be dissolved.

The reasons for believing that the doctrine of absolute indissolubility is neither traditional nor theologically proved have already been set out. It would seem, however, that the present proposal need not await a decision on that issue, because of the difference between and the separability of the concepts of sacramental marriage and valid civil contract.[1] A marriage contract

[1] See p. 137ff.

which fulfills the conditions stipulated in the civil law for validity is a civilly valid contract. What is suggested is that the Christian community accept the validity of that union, with all the moral, legal and social consequences. To do this, it is not directly necessary to pronounce on the religious value of the new marriage. Acceptance of its status can precede a decision regarding its sacramental nature, and is independent of that decision.

4. Dissolution of the marriage bond should cause no great shock to theologians. Ecclesiastical practice, as noted frequently in this book, permits the dissolution of the "natural" bond, and also of the sacramental bond in the case of a non-consummated marriage of Christians. Habit has made these facts so commonplace that their transcendent importance is easily overlooked. As regards the sacramental bond in particular, its complete dissolution was granted at first only when one spouse joined a religious order, and it is established that in many cases the marriages dissolved were actually consummated ones. If a special custom succeeded in this way in building up a solid tradition for an exception to the doctrine of absolute indissolubility of sacramental marriage, there is no reason to say that a new step in the matter of exceptions is impossible. The solidity of tradition is here incontestable. If the Greek Fathers and many of the Latins are agreed on any issue, it is in admitting the right of the innocent party—or at least the innocent husband—to remarry. For the Church, the authority of some of the great doctors of antiquity should suffice to justify the adoption of a humane and Christlike practice in favor of unfortunate spouses. Rigid and intransigent rules are hard to justify in Christianity. Mercy and understanding belong by right.

5. Modern logic offers a theory of scientific validity based on the method known as "testing." Here the procedure is not to show the truth of the elements of a scientific system, but specifically to establish the simple fact that no element of the system contradicts a verifiable and immediate empiric datum. If a statement deduced from the principles of the theory contradicts a verified fact, the theory has been "falsified."[2]

[2] See Karl R. Popper, *Logic of Scientific Discovery* (New York, Basic Books, 1959).

Application of this concept of validity to the theological-historical-canonical theory of marriage establishes that in frequent and foreseeable situations, celibacy is imposed on Christians against their will. But such obligatory celibacy contradicts true Christian teaching. The conclusion is clear. The theoretic system of Catholic marriage does not stand up.

To go more fully into the issue, the first thing to show is that the situation of the abandoned spouse is frequent, foreseeable, and sociologically relevant. It must be more than an exceptional case of the kind that the law cannot be expected to take into account. From the very foundation of the Church, this category of Christians has existed and had been the object of special disciplinary prescriptions. Today, it enjoys a special legal status. The determining element in this status is the marriage bond joining them to a guilty spouse who has left them. They cannot live together, yet the bond is ruled indissoluble, so that those bound by it cannot enter a new union. Moral laws meanwhile forbid sex relationships outside marriage. The result is that their legal status imposes the obligation of perfect continence for their entire life, or until the guilty spouse dies.

This obligation of perfect continence is explicitly affirmed by Catholic authors who discuss the situation. Bernard Häring speaks of "those divorced persons who have remarried civilly and who have not yet succeeded in controlling their appetites and imposing continence on themselves."[3] The same author offers this disturbing passage: "Everyone needs affection. If your neighbor is denied Christian love, he will try to get affection in a new marriage, although this will, of course, not be valid. Nor should we forget that suicide statistics show how exposed divorced persons are to fall into a state of desperation."[4]

The precept of absolute continence is often disguised as a gentle invitation. "If they begin to doubt," writes Cardinal Journet, "if they say that they are not saints, that they never sought this kind of life, that this cannot be their destiny, the Church

---

[3] *Le chrétien et le mariage* (Paris, 1965), p. 116.
[4] *Marriage in the Modern World* (Westminster, Md.: The Newman Press, 1965).

will answer that it can well be that they had not sought it before these unhappy experiences descended on them, but that they can desire it after what has happened, and that when God opens a road for the faithful soul, it is not in order to let him die on the way but to carry him to the end."[5]

These and other available texts make one point clear. The Church knows that it is demanding perfect continence from these members of the faithful who insist in the clearest terms that they feel no vocation for it. Yet the gospels and the epistles of St. Paul describe celibacy as a state to be freely chosen, insisting that its meritorious qualities derive precisely from this absolute freedom. Jesus says that "not all men can receive this precept, but only those to whom it is given" (Mt 19:11). And while Clement of Alexandria understands this to mean that the abandoned spouse is advised but not obliged to remain continent,[6] the modern discipline of the West understands that abandonment means for the innocent party a kind of irresistible and obligatory vocation to the state of perfect continence. However, neither Christian tradition nor theology can justify such a vocation.

Imposed celibacy has run counter to the Christian conscience at all times. Even in periods when the influence of encratism was great, efforts were always made to safeguard the absolute freedom of choice of the state of celibacy, as can be seen for example by reading the correspondence of Clement and Pinitos in the works of Eusebius of Cesarea.[7] The situation of the innocent abandoned spouses, nevertheless, does not seem to have occupied the attention of the Church's leaders since the establishment of the regime of Christendom. But in other surroundings the problem has been formulated in all its acuteness. When the ecclesiastical laws of England were being revised in the 17th century, the legislators offered this explanation of their reasons for changing the rule forbidding remarriage of the innocent spouse. "When one spouse is condemned for adultery, the innocent party may re-

---

[5] "Le mariage indissoluble," *La Documentation Catholique*, 63 (1966), col. 1083.
[6] See p. 96, above.
[7] See quotation from Clement on p. 86, above.

marry, at will. An innocent person should certainly not be punished for the crime of another, and celibacy is not to be imposed on one who does not desire it."[8]

Admittedly, the ups-and-downs of life call for observance of continence in many circumstances, or at least prevent marriage. Obvious situations of this kind arise in illness, during war, or when one is in jail. But in all such cases there is present the factor of physical necessity or moral culpability. Neither factor applies in the case of the innocent abandoned spouse. He is not culpable, and the law that claims to bind him is purely disciplinary, although it is buttressed by dogmatic claims. In a word, we have here an obligation of celibacy imposed against the will of the individual in virtue of religious principles of more than doubtful validity.

6. Recent pastoral reflection has resulted in a straightforward formulation of this issue. In examining the situation, the pastoral writers do not ignore any aspect, no matter how unpleasant. Here we are dealing with the data of sociological investigation. Bernard Häring, who has been quoted several times already, gives some pastoral rules for dealing with divorced and remarried persons. He starts with a realistic recognition of the fact by saying that "it would be incorrect and unjust simply to call such unions concubinage."[9] Similarly, the secretary general of the conference of French bishops describes the problems of the separated woman very realistically. "Material difficulties are combined with moral sufferings. The woman who refuses to remarry almost always turns in on herself in a solitude that increases day by day. She fears to say what she is thinking and locks herself in her room. This mood is intensified by the fact that in modern society a woman without a husband is treated with little consideration and is the object of improper proposals. She can easily reach a condition of nervous depression or even take her own life. Some women in this situation decide to remarry, and this provides once more the equilibrium of a conjugal union, restores them to

[8] *Reformatio legum ecclesiasticarum,* Chapter 5 "De adulterio et divortio," London, 1641. See Joyce, p. 627.
[9] *Op. cit.*

a proper place in society, and frees them from money worries."[10]
What is surprising is that such trivial remedies should be suggested for such great evils. They seem to think that such placebos as integration into a parish community, a club where those involved can give each other emotional support, or a gracious permission to the remarried to receive the sacraments occasionally in secret, can compensate for the lifelong deprivation of a fundamental human right. Yet doctrinal prejudgments close off the authentic pastoral sense which would make the spiritual guides of the community join with the abandoned spouses in a cry for freedom from legalistic obstacles preventing these goodliving Christians from taking the road to remaking their life by means of a new marriage. But the traditions of the schools and the intricacies of abstract thought continue to carry more weight with the leaders of the Church than do the demands of the reality of our times. Among Archbishop Zoghby's correspondence is a pathetic letter from a South American Catholic setting out his plight to his own bishop, along with the answer of the bishop, which in its entirety reads: "The request to remarry because of abandonment by the other spouse lacks theological and canonical basis." Did the situation not indicate a reply inspired a little more by the attitude of the one who had compassion on the multitudes? A bishop cannot change the canonical rules, but he can surely present to those higher up, with appropriate vigor, the problems he is unable to resolve because of the inadequacy of the laws.

Churchmen with deeply human feelings cannot fail to be disturbed by the extent of this problem. Cardinal Roncalli, the future Pope John, was such an ecclesiastic. It was natural for him to say what he said, as he was visiting French friends, while nuncio in Paris: "The problem of those who are separated—the Church must take action on that question."[11] Cardinal Roncalli knew perfectly well that the spokesmen of the Church claimed that it was taken care of already, and that no remarriage was pos-

[10] "Les divorcés non remariés et les femmes separées" in *La Documentation Catholique*, 64 (1967), col. 1712.
[11] From Archbishop Zobhby's correspondence. See p. 45, above.

sible. But in a man of God, faith and confidence can reach farther than the theology manuals.

7. The ecumenical climate in which Catholicism is living since Vatican Council II constitutes an urgent invitation to the Church to declare open various questions which had been considered definitively resolved in the closed atmosphere in which theology functioned since Trent. Indissolubility of marriage is such a question. To restudy this teaching is particularly important for relations with the Orthodox Churches whose discipline allows divorce on the basis of a tradition derived from the words of Jesus in St. Matthew's Gospel. Catholics have no choice but to respect the doctrinal and canonical criteria of the Orthodox. The ancient books venerated by the Eastern Churches as the foundation of their disciplines cannot be rejected as "impious" merely because they contain rules different from or contrary to those of the Latin Church.[12]

A sincere approach to the Eastern tradition on marriage and divorce presupposes a relativization of the Catholic attitude in the sense that it cannot be presented any longer as the sole authentic and legitimate interpretation of the words of Christ and the apostles on the subject. The continuing Catholic intransigence on this issue, even when modern needs have increased the tension almost unbearably, can be explained only by what must be recognized as moral reasons, namely, that the Roman Catholic Church considers divorce as something bad in itself. That means bad not only for Catholics, but for all Christians and for all men. Such a position, however, is the equivalent of saying that the Orthodox and Protestant Churches support an institution that is gravely and publicly immoral. The fact that this is not stressed in ecumenical contacts does not mean that it is not implicit in the Roman position.

In addition, the Oriental tradition, maintained for so many centuries with few variations, constitutes an illuminating example for Catholics. It shows, first of all, that acceptance of divorce is compatible with the most sincere adherence to the revealed word

---

[12] For example, the *Nomocanon*, a collection of canon laws made in the 8th century, the object of many criticisms by Catholic writers.

and the traditions of the Church Fathers, both of which are, beyond question, characteristics of the Eastern Churches. It also shows that the dreadful disasters which Catholic moralists and canonists claim to be inseparable from the introduction of divorce have not happened in the East, but that on the contrary the sacramental value of marriage and the integrity of the family have been fully maintained. The point is an important one. The Christian East demonstrates in a practical way that the institution of divorce does not change in the slightest the structure of a moral, social and religious life inspired by the gospel teaching.

In the discipline of the East, the case of the innocent spouse abandoned or outraged by adultery on the part of the other spouse has a special category, one that might be called primary. The reason is that Eastern theologians explain the extension of divorce to other cases by assimilating them to that of adultery as the one deriving from the tradition of the Bible and the Church Fathers.

8. The eventual benefits which such a discipline might confer on the guilty party seem to weigh very heavily with many of the moralists who discuss the question. But what is needed here is a little common sense. It would be absurd not to give somebody what he deserves and needs simply because another undeserving person will share. The right of the innocent should not suffer the consequences of the lack of right of the guilty.

The proposal made here, however, confers no benefit on the guilty party. The Church does not play any part in the remarriage of the innocent spouse. It merely accepts it in the social and community areas. But the religious community does not accept the guilty one, because there is question of a public sinner. However, this does not mean that the new civil marriage of the guilty party is to be considered invalid. As repeatedly stated, it is not for the Church to make that judgment. But the Christian community cannot welcome a member who has offended publicly and gravely, unless he asks for reconciliation and does appropriate penance. In that case, he can be readmitted, because there is nothing to show that the sin of infidelity cannot be forgiven in this world. A guilty party who repents can consequently be accepted again by the community after a period of trial and penance.

III. CANONICAL IMPLICATIONS

The laws of Catholic morality, taken literally, describe remarriage of the innocent abandoned spouse as adultery and bigamy. Many authors call this union concubinage, although the legal definition restricts concubinage to a continuing relationship between unmarried persons. The adultery or concubinage is public, placing the parties in the category of public sinners.

Canon 2356 of the code of canon law sets out the penalties for bigamy. "Bigamists, that is to say, those who attempt another marriage—even a so-called civil one—while a marriage bond to prevent it exists, are ipso facto infamous. If they ignore the warning of the Ordinary and continue in their unlawful cohabitation, they are to be excommunicated or punished by personal interdict, according to the seriousness of the offense."[13]

Various restrictions are imposed on the infamous and on public sinners. Canon 855 provides: "They are to be excluded from the Eucharist who are publicly unworthy, as those who are excommunicated, interdicted, and those notoriously infamous, unless their repentance and amendment is publicly known and they have previously repaired the public scandal caused by them." The exclusion continues after death. "Public and manifest sinners . . . are to be denied Church burial, unless before death they shall have shown some sign of repentance" (Canon 1240). "A person deprived of Christian burial shall also be denied any funeral Mass, even an anniversary Mass, as well as all other public funeral services" (Canon 1241). The exclusion is extended to associations of the faithful by Canon 693: "Membership in an association is not open to . . . public sinners."

The formulations of these canons call to mind the dusty legal tomes of another era, but the practical impact is still felt by thousands of the Catholic faithful who find themselves classed as "public sinners" because of marriage irregularities they cannot correct. The letters reproduced earlier in this book express some of the

[13] Pope Paul VI's instruction, *Matrimonii sacramentum* (1966), eliminated the censure of excommunication which was previously incurred automatically by Catholics who remarried before a non-Catholic clergyman. See Canon 2319, 1.

suffering caused by the total exclusion from the life of the Christian community of those who contracted a civil marriage because denied a canonical one. All this would change, if the Church law would introduce the concept of a "valid civil marriage," as suggested above, without ruling on its religious standing and leaving its acceptance in particular cases to pastoral judgment. By recognizing the moral propriety of the remarriage, the limitations resulting from categorization as a public sinner would automatically disappear, and the situation would cease to be classed as bigamy.

The guilty party would naturally not enjoy these benefits and would continue to be excluded from the life of the Christian community. The terms of his exclusion should be left to a pastoral decision, however, because it is difficult for law to anticipate all circumstances and adjust its rulings accordingly. The community already possesses some simple rules for its pastoral guidance which have infinitely greater authority than the canonical codes: "So if you are offering your gift at the altar, and there remember that your brother has something against you, leave your gift there before the altar and go; first be reconciled to your brother, and then come and offer your gift" (Mt 5:23–24).

This position is quite distinct from that which Victor Pospishil calls "tolerance through dissimulation," and which he describes as follows: "Could not such Catholics be admitted to the sacraments, under the assumption that perhaps their marriages too are valid because of some general, canonical, undefinable ground of invalidity in respect to the first marriages? . . . The invalidity of the first marriage might not be determinable according to the man-made regulations of the Church; and therefore the inability of the legal system to satisfy what is right and just ought to be supplemented by a tolerant attitude towards such remarried members of the Church."[14]

---

[14] *Divorce and Remarriage* (New York: Herder & Herder, 1967), p. 119. Pospishil quotes from "The Tragedy of Broken Marriages," by Robert Adolfs, O.S.A., *Jubilee*, March 1966, pp. 46–48. Adolfs had written: "Fortunately, a much milder pastoral practice has been applied in recent years, in many dioceses. When it is definitely established that the first marriage bond has been completely severed, the local pastor may allow those married in a civil ceremony to receive sacraments in private. If the non-religious marriage of the pair in question is not known in the parish they

What is here proposed is not a mere pastoral tolerance but a new attitude of the Church presupposing the acceptance of certain postulates, for example, that the contract and the sacrament are not identical, that civil marriage can be valid, and that the faithful have the right in some circumstances to be married civilly. All this would not produce a "tolerated illegality" but a new legality.

The proposal requires the immediate acceptance of the category of valid civil marriage of baptized persons. It is an idea that caused jolts of deep horror to Catholics a century ago. But it flows inescapably from the right understanding of religious freedom proclaimed by the second Vatican Council. Every man, even if baptized, has the right to contract a lawful marriage without being subjected to religious conditions. The Church is consequently committed to recognizing a civil marriage of baptised persons which is valid and lawful yet not sacramental. The proposal made here is in this sense a strategic one. Starting from a position which the Church has publicly accepted in principle, it provides a quick and adequate solution for the problem of the innocent abandoned spouse.

IV. Practical and Pastoral Aspects

The right to enter a new marriage acceptable to the community belongs to the innocent abandoned spouse. Abandonment and innocence are expressions capable of legal definition. Abandonment of the conjugal home is an offense listed in all penal codes, and innocence is a matter for judicial determination in every case of separation or divorce. In practice, nevertheless, all cases are not crystal clear. On the contrary, one encounters a multitude of circumstances almost impossible to unravel, and the attitude of the religious community will not necessarily be the same as that of the civil court. Personal conscience carries more weight in the Christian community, although the external facts and their consequences cannot be ignored completely.

The concept of abandonment should be taken in a broad sense,

---

can even receive the sacraments in public. In any case, all cause of scandal must be eliminated." Anglican Bishop C. Gore had made a similar proposal in 1912. See Dupont, *Mariage et divorce dans l'Evangile*, p. 126, note 2.

in terms of the understanding of the community. The innocent spouse is often the one who leaves the conjugal home, because the other party has made life together impossible. In extreme cases, such as continued and obstinate adultery, the decision is clear. At other times, it is less easy to determine the nature of the abandonment. When that is so, the Christian community should be slow to give the seal of its approval to conduct that may later prove immoral. Time and the attitude of the other party may resolve the doubt.

Nevertheless, the proposal under study concerns the case of the abandoned spouse exclusively. It is not directly concerned with the issue of placing other similar situations on an equal footing, or with the attitude of the leaders of the Christian community toward a spouse who is having problems and seeks to separate or abandon the community of marriage.

Civil divorce is becoming the normal and recognized method for resolving or regularizing the situation of the innocent abandoned spouse.[15] The leaders of the religious community should advise and help members who find it necessary to seek divorce, giving them economic and legal aid as required. The fact that the new marriage is to be contracted only before the civil authorities does not by any means imply that it lacks religious worth. The second marriage can be seen as having a double religious value. First, it is a morally good act, inserted as such into the only economy of salvation that exists, that founded on Jesus Christ. But as a marriage, it has a special religious value. Every conjugal union represents the union of God with man, and every conjugal union of Christians recalls Christ's total giving of himself to the Church. When the need for grace proper to the new state is also remembered, the conclusion is inescapable that there are very many points of contact between this and a sacramental marriage. However, recognition of this near identity is not prerequisite to community acceptance of remarriage of the innocent abandoned spouse.

---

[15] A timid recognition of civil divorce is found in ecclesiastical legal practice. Since nullity decisions of the Holy See are not recognized by many governments, the parties are advised to get a civil divorce (See Abate, *Lo scioglimento*, p. 149).

With this starting point, pastoral practice might very well suggest a religious ceremony that would signify the acknowledgment by the Christian community of the religious values in the new union of two of its members. They might, for example, be put in a special place at the Sunday assembly, and the blessing of heaven might be invoked on them. This would be neither more nor less than a revival of the practice of Christians of the early centuries when two of them had married.

Whatever the fate of the immediate solution here presented, the problem of the innocent abandoned spouses will continue to call for an adequate and realistic answer. Decisions may be postponed, but they cannot be put off for ever. The Church is faced with a crisis which is becoming more acute and acquiring a clear form within the community. It is no longer simply an external question involving changes of organization or of political stands. The problem is fundamentally pastoral and religious, and the Church leaders can study and resolve it without the fear of significant unfavorable reaction. In the final analysis, what is at issue is perhaps a challenge to faith. The faithful who are suffering because of the inadequacy of current Church legislation are suffering precisely because of their faith, and that is the major contribution they are making at this time. The Church leaders, who are not suffering this drama in their own flesh, should give the highest proof of their confidence in God by making a substantial change in discipline without waiting for the assurances—which are always only human—of the theologians and canonists. If the faith of those who decide is joined to the faith of those who hope, the drama of the abandoned will cease to be such, and one more testimony will have been given to the world.

Appendix

Archbishop Zoghby's interventions at Vatican Council II.

1. September 29, 1965. There is a far more agonizing problem than birth control, that of the innocent partner left completely alone, without any fault on his part and while still young, because of the adultery of the other. The marriage seemed a happy one, but quite soon one spouse—through human weakness or with premeditation—abandons the home and enters a new union. The innocent one goes to his pastor or bishop, but the answer is always the same. "I can do nothing for you. Pray, and resign yourself to living alone and observing continence for the rest of your life." It is a solution that presupposes heroic virtue, rare faith and a very uncommon temperament. It is therefore not for everyone.

The young man or woman who had married because he or she had not felt a call to perpetual continence is thus driven often to a new unlawful union outside the Church to keep from becoming neurotic. Such honest and typical Catholics are reduced to living with a tormented conscience. They were left with a single choice, either to become exceptional Christians overnight or perish.

We know perfectly well that perpetual continence is not a solution for the average Christian. In other words, we know that we are leaving these young victims without an answer. We ask them to rely on a faith that works miracles, although miracle-working faith is not given to everyone. Even many of ourselves, the bishops of the Church, have still to struggle and pray a great deal before we can hope to obtain it.

The question these tortured souls are submitting to the Council today is this. Has the Church the right to tell an innocent member, no matter what the nature of the problem torturing him: "Work it out for yourself, because I have no solution for your situation"? Or can the Church at best here offer an exceptional solution which it knows can work only for exceptional persons?

The Church has certainly received from Christ sufficient authority to offer all its children means of salvation proportionate to their strength, as of course aided by divine grace. Heroism and the state of perfection were never imposed by Christ under threat of damnation. "If you wish to be perfect," Christ said. "If you *wish* it. . . ."

The Church, in consequence cannot lack the authority required to protect the innocent spouse against the consequences of the sin of the other spouse. It does not seem normal that perpetual continence, something pertaining to the state of perfection, can be imposed as an obligation and a punishment on an innocent and betrayed partner.

The Eastern churches have always been aware that they possess this authority, and they have always exercised it in favor of the innocent spouse. It is true that the bond of marriage has been made indissoluble by the positive law of Christ, but—as St. Matthew's gospel indicates (5:32; 19:6)—"except in case of adultery." It is for the church to judge the meaning of this phrase. If the church of Rome has always interpreted it restrictively, the same was not the case in the East, where from the first centuries the church interpreted it in favor of the possibility of remarriage for the innocent spouse.

It is true that the Council of Trent, at its 24th session (*De Matrimonio*, canon 7), approved the restrictive Roman interpretation. But it is well known that the formula adopted by the Council in this canon had been deliberately rephrased so as not to exclude the Eastern tradition of a practice contrary to that of Rome. The credit is due to the speakers from Venice who were familiar with the Greek tradition, a tradition based on the interpretation of the Greek Fathers, and also on that of some Western Fathers, including St. Ambrose of Milan.

We know how the Fathers of the Eastern Church tried to dissuade widowers and widows from remarrying, following in this the advice of the Apostle. But they never wanted to deprive the innocent spouse, unjustly abandoned, of the right to remarry. This tradition retained in the East, and never disapproved during ten centuries of union, could today be taken back and adopted by Catholics. Progress of patristic studies in recent times has directed new attention to the Eastern Fathers. Both as exegetes and as moralists, they were just as good as those of the West.

The Western canonists have been led by their pastoral concern to take a different approach to the problem of people with marriage difficulties. Using a casuistry so subtle that it sometimes seems a form of gymnastics, they try to unearth all sorts of impediments capable of invalidating the marriage contract. Their motive has undoubtedly been pastoral concern, but the results have at times been harmful to souls. For example, sometimes after ten or twenty years of marriage, a previously unsuspected impediment of affinity is discovered, and this provides a magic solution for everything. The jurists regard this as natural and normal, but we pastors should realize that the faithful are at times shocked and scandalized.

The already mentioned tradition of the Eastern Fathers is surely better suited than these marriage impediments as a way to exercise the divine mercy in favor of Christian spouses. I agree that one must decide prudently. Abuses are always possible, but the abuse of authority does not destroy the authority itself.

In this time of ecumenism and dialogue, I hope that the Catholic Church can come to recognize the age-old tradition of the Eastern Church. I hope, too, that the theologians will dedicate themselves to the study of this problem, to provide a remedy for the anguish of innocent abandoned spouses and to rescue them from the danger that gravely threatens their salvation.

2. October 4, 1965. As certain publications read an unduly wide meaning into my recent Council intervention about the particular case—a frequent and sad one—of the innocent abandoned spouse, and as they distributed the text of the intervention all round the world, I have requested the opportunity, not to take back or change what I then said, but to note briefly some points.

1. My intervention had a single purpose, a strictly pastoral one. That was to find a solution for the problem of so many young husbands and wives who are condemned to live alone, in compulsory continence, through no fault of their own.

2. I affirmed clearly in my intervention the immutable principle of the indissolubility of marriage, and I deliberately avoided using the word *divorce*, a word which in Catholic usage means the breach of the immutable principle of the indissolubility of marriage.

3. This indissolubility of marriage is so deeply rooted in the tradition of the churches of the East and of the West, both Orthodox and Catholic, that it could not be called in question in an intervention at the Council. The Orthodox tradition has always considered marriage to be indissoluble, as indissoluble as the union of Christ with the church, his spouse, a union which is the exemplary model of the monogamous and sacramental union of Christians. Orthodox theology regards divorce as merely a dispensation granted the innocent party, in clearly defined cases and in the context of a purely pastoral concern. It is given by virtue of what the Orthodox call "the principle of economy," meaning a dispensation or rather an exercise of condescension. This dispensation does not exclude the principle of the indissolubility of marriage. On the contrary, it protects the principle, in the same way as the dispensations from valid and consummated marriages granted by the Catholic Church in virtue of the Petrine privilege. We will not talk about the abuses, which are always possible, but which do not change the theological reality.

4. In consequence, what I suggested in my intervention was a dispensation in favor of the innocent spouse. Referring to the traditional interpretation in the East of St. Matthew's text, I envisaged the possibility that the Catholic Church might add to the grounds for dispensation it already recognizes that of fornication and the desertion of one spouse by the other, thereby removing the danger that the innocent party may lose his soul. This dispensation no more threatens the principle of indissolubility of marriage than do those already admitted.

5. This is not a frivolous suggestion. On the contrary, it is

based on the unquestioned authority of saintly Fathers and Doctors of the Eastern Churches, and it would be temerarious to charge them with having yielded to political and human considerations when they interpreted the words of the Lord in the way they did.

6. Within this framework of absolute fidelity on the part of both the East and the West to the principle of the indissolubility of marriage, the Roman Church never questioned, during the long centuries of union or after separation, the legitimacy of the Eastern discipline permitting remarriage of the innocent spouse. The Western Church itself, including some popes and various Latin councils, practised the same tolerance up to the 12th century.

Conclusion
Such is the sense of my recent Council intervention. We have here an exegetical, canonical and pastoral problem that we should not toss aside. As for the opportuneness of admitting a new ground for dispensation, analogous to those already introduced in virtue of the Petrine privilege, that is a matter for the Church's judgment.

Bibliography

Chapter 2
Alves, Joseph T., "Consequences of Marriage Breakdown," in *Marriage: a Psychological and Moral Approach*, W. C. Bier ed., New York, Fordham University Press, 1965.
Crespy, G., Eudokimov, P., Duquoc, Christian, *Le Mariage*, Tours, Mame, 1967.
Fortuna-Jorio-Pandini, *Rapporto sul divorzio in Italia*, Milan, Sugar, 1966.
Glick, Paul C., *American Families: a volume in the Census Monograph Series*, New York, 1957.
Goode, William J., *After Divorce*, Glencoe, Ill., The Free Press, 1959.
Häring, Bernard, *Marriage in the Modern World*, Westminster, Maryland, Newman, 1965.
Pospishil, Victor J., *Divorce and Remarriage*, New York, Herder & Herder, 1967.
Schillebeeckx, Edward, *Marriage, Human Reality and Saving Mystery*, New York, Sheed & Ward, 1965.

Chapter 3
Barton, J. M. T., *The New Testament and Divorce*, Dublin, 1934.
Crespy, Georges, "Sur la grâce du marriage" in *Le Mariage*, Tours, Mame, 1967.
Dupont, Jacques, *Mariage et divorce dans l'Evangile*, Bruges, Abbaye de Saint-André, 1959.
Souarn, R., "L'adultère et le lien du mariage d'après l'Ecriture Sainte," in *Dictionnaire de Théologie Catholique*, Vol. I, Paris, Letouzey et Ané, 1909, cols. 468–475.
Vogt, Fritz, *Das Ehegesetzt Jesu*, Freiburg, 1936.

Chapter 4

Arendzen, J. P., "Ante-Nicene Interpretations of the Sayings on Divorce," in *Journal of Theological Studies*, 20 (1919) pp. 230–241.

Bonsirven, J., "Nisi ob fornicationem: éxegèse primitive," in *Mélanges Ferdinand Cavallera*, Toulouse, pp. 47–63.

Esmein, E., and Genestal, R., *Le mariage en droit canonique*, Paris, 1935.

Fahrner, Ignaz, *Geschichte des Unauflösigkeitsprinzips und der vollkommenen Scheidung der Ehe im kanonischen Recht*, Freiburg, 1903.

Freisen, E., *Geschichte des katholischen Eherechts bis zum Verfall der Glossenliteratur*, Paderborn, Schöningh, 1963.

Hefele-Leclercq, *Histoire des Conciles*, vol. 3, Paris, Letouzey et Ané, 1909.

Joyce, George H., *Christian Marriage*, London, 1948.

Mayaud, J. B. M., *L'indissolubilité du mariage: étude historico-canonique*, Strasbourg and Paris, 1952.

Ott, A., *Die Auslegung der neutestamentlichen Texte über die Ehescheidung, historisch-kritisch dargestellt*, Neutestamentliche Abhandlungen, book III, 1–3, Münster, 1911.

Perrone, G., *De Matrimonio Cristiano*, vol. 3, Rome, 1858.

Preisker, H., *Christentum und Ehe in den ersten drei Jahrhunderten*, Berlin, 1927.

Turmel, J., *Histoire des Dogmes*, vol. 3, pp. 529–569, Paris, 1936.

Vacant, A., "Adultère (L') et le lien du mariage dans l'Eglise Latine du V au XVI siècle," in *Dictionnaire de Théologie Catholique*, I, Paris, Letouzey et Ané, 1909, cols, 484–498.

Chapter 5

Abate, Antonio, *Lo scioglimento del vincolo coniugale*, Rome, 1965.

Adnès, P., *Le Mariage*, Tournai, Desclée, 1963.

Crespy, G., Eudokimov, P., Duquoc, Ch., *Le Mariage*, Tours, Mame, 1967.

David, J. *Nouveaux aspects de la doctrine catholique du mariage*, (translated from German), Paris, 1967.

Daubercies, P., *La condition charnelle. Recherches positives pour la théologie d'une realité terrestre*, Tours, Mame, 1959.

Häring, Bernard, *Marriage in the Modern World*, Westminster, Maryland, Newman, 1965.

Joyce, George H., *Christian Marriage*, London, 1948.

Leclercq, H., "Mariage," in *Dictionnaire d'Archéologie chrétienne et de Liturgie*, Paris, 1907–1952, vol. 10.

Rondet, Henri, *Introduction à l'étude de la théologie du mariage*, Paris, P. Lethielleux, 1960.

Index